THE PURSUIT OF PEACE SCIENCE, LAW, AND ART

THE PURSUIT OF PEACE SCIENCE, LAW, AND ART

BASED ON A TRUE STORY OF TWO REMARKABLE PEOPLE AND ART TREASURE

Anthony R. Wells

CONTENTS

DEDICATION

This book is dedicated to all those throughout the world who work constantly to preserve peace at a time of Global conflict. It reflects the urgent need to combine the strengths of all those generous and truly noble people throughout the world irrespective of their country, race, color, religion, positions in life, and philosophical disposition, who seek daily to prevent the worst of all human behavior manifest in crimes against humanity, war crimes, and those who practice the many forms of discrimination and abuse against their fellow human beings.

This is a book about hope founded in the manifest lives and work of people who strive to do that which is right, rendering unto no man or woman evil for evil, rather helping the fainthearted, supporting the weak, honoring all people, and being of good cheer in situations of hardship, tragedy, and despair, through their innate kindness and faith in the inner goodness of most people.

It is also dedicated to those who have the grave responsibility to seek out and pursue the worst forms of human abuse and makes special recognition of the International Criminal Court (ICC), the International Court of Justice, and the European Court of Human Rights. The Peace Palace in The Hague, Netherlands, is the main judicial organ of the United Nations, the home of the International Court of Justice, the main judicial organ of the United Nations. This book recognizes the hope for peace manifest in these institutions in addition to the myriad people throughout the world who work constantly to use their many talents and dedication to the pursuit of peace.

PREFACE

2022-2023 witnessed tragedies on a huge scale precipitated by human weakness, folly, and wickedness, exacerbated by nature that caused catastrophic earthquakes, hurricanes, floods, and destruction and loss of life on enormous scales. Dominating this era of destruction was the February, 2022 Russian invasion of Ukraine followed in October, 2023 by a Middle East crisis and war of enormous proportions. These events brought into sharp focus the precipitous, reckless, and thoroughly evil actions of a relatively very small number of human beings that led and instigated actions that have caused the deaths of hundreds of thousands of innocent human beings, caught up in events not of their choosing. The sum of the parts make the whole, and each of us, each individual can make a difference. We can collectively change the world for the better, countering the evil worst intentions and actions of those who precipitate death, destruction, and human suffering on enormous scales. History is replete with those who made a difference and showed and led the way to peace and harmony. This story is about how two individuals, in totally widely different ways, can make a difference. To these two lives is added the dimension of a crucial human endeavor that has marked our progress and development since the earliest times, the role of art as a human virtue, a creative life form that underlies humankind's ability to come to terms with our existence and our progress through time. The art aspect is very different, seen through the lens of good and bad, and unified in the theme of achieving peace and that which is right after turmoil, and downright evil.

The story challenges us to review our world, and what each of us may do to enhance peace, to look beyond the daily routine that most of us follow by the sheer nature of our circumstances and find ways and means by which we may all contribute, albeit perhaps in small, maybe insignificant ways in the greater scheme of things, though nonetheless significant. The reason is simple. Each of us can make a difference in our own individual way, and together, collectively, the sum of us all can truly make a huge difference. The pursuit of peace is not an imagery ideal. It is a fundamental necessity that behooves us all to help maintain for the sake of our world, children, grandchildren and all those whom we love and care about. This story is about hope and how peace can be shaped by positive and courageous human endeavor.

CAST OF MAIN CHARACTERS

There are two main characters and an abstract character in the form of Art. Outstanding Art has a unifying effect globally, irrespective of its origins and with whatever country of origin, culture, religion, or ethnic background. Art has not only its own unique character it also has a history of ownership. Art fits into a much wider worldview of what is right and how peace can be achieved through reconciling what is right with past wrongs.

The two characters are Claude Frank Riley, Junior (hereafter simply Claude Riley) and Benjamin Ferencz (hereafter Ben Ferencz). Neither of these men knew each other. Claude lived from 1922-2012, aged 92 at his passing, and Benjamin from March 11, 1920- April 7, 2023. Ben Ferencz was 103 when he passed away, lucid and wise until shortly before his passing.

Both men lived remarkable lives, Ben perhaps much more widely known internationally and revered for his contributions to peace and the maintenance of international order and justice. He established his position in history as a very young man as a lead prosecutor at the Nuremberg War Crimes trials. Claude, less well known, though distinguished for his achievements, was a young World War Two scientist, born two years apart from Ben, so very much of the same generation, who during and after World War Two made significant contributions to science and technology, largely unknown to most people.

Their lives and work reflect very different aspects and ways in which the peace of the world can be maintained and improved. Both men's lives demonstrate that through outstanding professionalism, education, innovation, courage, and resilience, guided by value system that upholds human dignity and freedom, the world can become a better place. In the midst of chaos, often horrendous evil and barbarous actions, their lives show how decency, freedom and, most of all, peace may be maintained, at times against all odds.

Art reflects the human condition and aspirations throughout time. Art illustrates in this story how peace and justice may uphold all that is good in our world, how decency and that which is right may be pursued against the worst of human actions. Together the two main characters and art combine to show that in our challenging world there is always hope and always a way forward to preserve peace. The pursuit of peace may be achieved by myriad means. This story shows how two men contributed to our peace and why it is essential that their lives, achievements, and values encourage us all to follow in their footsteps and pursue peace.

LIGHT SHINES ON THE DARKEST HOURS

None of us know what life will bring as we enter this world as whatever, whether the child of the well-to-do or the impoverished, or something and everything in between. We are all whatever the fate of our place and nature of birth dictate. Our innate selves combine with our environment to influence and control our development. A myriad range of different factors, forces, events, people, and geography combine to place us where we are, at that one moment in time. It's our unique inflection point, not ours necessarily to control until later in life, yet for whatever reasons of circumstance it is where we are, all that we can be right there and then, Life is what we all make it. None of us control the environment into which we are born and none of us know what is really happening around us, let alone globally, until later when we become very much our unique selves. What happens next is so important. The "Next" is when we all as unique individuals become rounded people, yes influenced by our environment and family, though still a real person with a personality and attitude to life that can be influenced both positively and negatively. We have all been there. Growing up is what we call the maturation process. How that occurs and how we develop can be largely in our own hands if we are fortunate enough to have guiding parents, family, and teachers. The world is our oyster, and it can also be our challenge if the more positive, dare one say, nobler aspects of the human condition are not encouraged and followed. There are many crossroads as we mature, many choices, many opportunities, and also many pitfalls. Into life's post World War One world arrived Claude Riley, born on April 24th, 1922.

When Claude died aged 90 in 2012 he had witnessed ninety years of enormous change. In 1922 he knew nothing of the state of the world and what was needed to ensure that the world would hopefully never again witness the horrors and incredible loss of life in Europe, ravaged by a war that was called "The War to End all Wars". The child became a man. The 1920s saw the nations of the world attempt to avoid another massive confrontation on the scale of the 1914-1918 war. As a young person Claude could barely comprehend what the League of Nations entailed and why it was formed, to maintain peace amongst nations and deter war, and how the Great Depression precipitated in 1929 would shock a world still rebuilding itself after conflict eleven years earlier.

Each of us in our own unique individual ways can make a difference, whatever the nature, scale, significance and worth of that difference. It does not matter how and why each of us moves through life to do whatever it is that we do. There has to be something else beyond material success, status, recognition, and pure human gain to perhaps make our lives truly meaningful. The latter is for each of us to decide our way of life, to judge what balance to seek and maintain, and to find within the often non controllable factors that influence our lives a way ahead that creates a sense of well being, to be the best we can, and perhaps to find joy and happiness even when life may not be offering the best of times.

Claude Riley spent ninety fine years figuring out what not only made him personally happy. He grew to find through the huge challenges facing our world during his ninety years that there were certain values and goals in life that supplant perhaps many of the worldly and material aspects that so often control why, how, and what we each do with our one precious life on this planet. Perhaps the biggest single factor that at life's end Claude regarded as the most precious beyond the love of family and friends was very simply the creation and maintenance of "Peace". He recognized that a world without peace is and can become a world full of misery and human suffering that defies both reason and what he felt was the innate goodness of all human beings that accept, and practice, the rights of all us to live in peace. Naivety, perhaps combined with lack of worldliness, let alone ignorance of history, may indeed inhibit a realistic and practical approach to addressing often enormous human differences. Claude was to exhibit over ninety years that there is always hope, always a way forward, that peace is always possible, and though this may come sometimes at huge cost, it is always a much better to the alternatives, all too often characterized by despotism, tyranny, human suffering on enormous scales, and downright evil.

Peace comes at a price.

Claude Riley's life shows just one dimension, through science and technology, how peace can be maintained as long as the intentions are right as judged by value systems that have stood the test of time.

The 1930s in Europe witnessed the darkest of hours, with the rise of Hitler and Nazi Germany, and in Asia the challenge from an imperialist and expansionist Japan combined to destroy the goodness for Peace that the League of Nations had been formed to guarantee. In September, 1939 when war began in Europe after the Nazi invasion of Poland Claude was just seventeen years of age and when the Japanese attacked the US Pacific Fleet at Pearl Harbor on December 7, 1941 he was a mere nineteen years of age. He was about to be precipitated into the most devastating war that the world had witnessed. Peace had gone. Europe was overrun and occupied by Nazi German, other than fascist Spain and a Portugal that maintained neutrality under its leader, Antonio de Oliveira Salazar.

The lights had gone out and 1940 saw the stand alone British facing devastating bombing of their cities by the German Luftwaffe. Into these darkest of times young Claude Riley began his contribution to restoring peace through war, the only alternative to capitulation and subjugation to tyranny and the despotic rule of evil nations. Peace would come at enormous cost. These were the darkest of years yet there still shone the beacons of hope encapsulated in Britain's stand alone "Finest Hour" followed by the United States commitment to end tyranny, all consummated on August 14th, 1941, just a few months before the Japanese attack on Pearl Harbor, with the meeting of President Franklin Roosevelt and Prime Minister Winston Churchill. They met on board the Royal Navy battleship Prince of Wales, highly secretly, in Placentia Bay, off Newfoundland, the President having sailed secretly in USS Augusta from Washington DC. They agreed on the way ahead to destroy Nazism and liberate Europe, and sharing valuable intelligence. Pearl Harbor was a few months away and soon both nations would be joined militarily in the challenge of a two front global confrontation.

Where would Claude Riley fit into this scheme of things? Would peace prevail?

One young man caught up in a deluge of violence and threats to the very existence of the United States and the way of life of the world's greatest democracy, supporting now its one great ally, the United Kingdom and its Dominions.

TWO

THE YOUNG ENGINEER ENTERS THE FRAY

After December 7, 1941 the world changed for the people of the United States. Many young Americans would not live to see peace in 1945, giving their lives for freedom and to preserve the goodness of the American way of life and all that was dear to them and their families. When Claude Frank Riley, Junior, was born in Milledgeville, Georgia, on April 24, 1922 his parents could not have envisaged that between 1943 and 1946 their son would be a First Lieutenant in the US Army Air Corps (the predecessor to the United States Air Force, founded in 1947), along with millions of other American young men. Claude received his education in Georgia. He obtained an Arts Associate degree from Georgia Military College in 1942, followed in 1943 by a BS in General Engineering from the Georgia Institute of Technology. After World War Two he did graduate work in Mathematics and Physics 1946-1947 at Cornell University, and completed an MS in Aeronautical Engineering from the University of Michigan in 1949. He became a Licensed Professional Engineer in three states, Illinois, Maryland, and New York. He would spend the whole of his professional life in a wide variety of distinguished positions in a variety of major American high technology corporations as well as being the founder and manager of independent scientific and industrial enterprises. Claude knew how to manage and lead as well as innovate scientifically. He contributed significantly, for example, to the growth and development of Booz, Allen, & Hamilton, along with several other renowned US companies, such as Tracor, Inc, Auerbach Associates, Inc, and the Bell Aircraft Company. In 1943 family connections assisted the young Claude. Carl Vinson, the Chairman of the US House of Representatives Committee on Naval Affairs, helped him gain access to the right technical people in the US War Department. In a letter dated September 20, 1943 Carl Vinson wrote to his father, ending, "Let me assure you that it is always a pleasure for me to do whatever I can for you and your son. With highest personal regards I remain, Sincerely your friend, Carl Vinson". This set in train the beginning of a long career where the most significant and innovative science and technologies were developed and put in the service of the United States. Claude was destined to become part of the American community that would lead innovation in the service of the defense of the United States and its Allies. Through the life of one human being we gain insight into the critical role of science in the pursuit of peace. World War Two placed huge demands on the US science and technology community. Faced with the overwhelming onslaught in the early years of conflict of both Nazi and Japanese aggression the US leadership with its principal and enduring ally, the United Kingdom, faced many inevitable moral questions about technology, war, and the inevitable destruction of human life that war brought and demanded in order that victory could be achieved. Peace would come at enormous cost in human life. The young Claude was thrown into this challenge with millions more young Americans together with the older generation who would provide the leadership and strategy that would lead to ultimate victory. The latter demanded that science and technology stay not only ahead of the enemy and also that it would make a difference, by both saving American lives and ensuring that the enemies strategic capability to continue war was undermined to the point of destruction. The United States and the United Kingdom worked together to ensure that the Nazi and Japanese industrial base and war machines were destroyed while in parallel providing the front line forces, on the ground, in the air, and at sea with overwhelming capabilities that outmatched the enemy. Science and technology in the service of peace flourished because of the sheer urgency of the situation. A "Just War" as defined by international legal scholars, and today reinforced in the tenets and organizations of the United Nations and the Geneva Conventions, provides the moral framework for defense against aggression against the sovereignty of states. Nazi Germany and Japan provoked and pursed war that created the legal justification for a "Just War". The latter required the talents and skills of American and British science and technology.

From his World War Two role and experience as a very junior member of the Manhattan project team Claude Riley would move into a diverse field of technical innovation in the post World War Two era. From November, 1943 to June, 1946, while in the US Army Air Corps, he did innovative work at the Power Plant Laboratory at Wright Field, in Dayton, Ohio. He was here that the young Riley was introduced to the highly classified work in support of the Manhattan atomic weapons project led by J. Robert Oppenheimer at the secret facility at Los Alamos, near Santa Fe, New Mexico, established in 1943 for designing the first nuclear weapon, atomic bomb, culminating in the first live test under the direction of General Leslie Groves and J. Robert Oppenheimer. Claude Riley's team and work contributed to the work of the Los Alamos facility, with the first nuclear test near Alamogordo, New Mexico, codename : "Trinity", on July, 16, 1945, prior to the two weapons "Little Boy" and "Fat Man" used in the attacks on Hiroshima and Nagasaki. The work that was done at Los Alamos continued after World War Two in conjunction with the Lawrence Livermore National Laboratory that was placed by the US government under the direction of the University of California Berkeley. Both national Laboratories ensured that the United States and its allies stayed ahead in the nuclear era and provided the critical technical means by which the MAD (Mutual Assured Destruction) doctrine endured through and until the end of the Cold War. Peace was maintained by outstanding science. Today both National Laboratories have expanded their research and development into many non nuclear multidisciplinary research fields that include space exploration, nuclear fusion, renewable energy, medicine, nanotechnology, and supercomputing. Lawrence Livermore recently demonstrated new and innovative means to create electricity, completely different from all conventional methods, that may help over time resolve the urgent need to generate electricity to support the myriad systems and technologies associated for example with electric vehicles. Claude Riley was invited to address many key technical problems from the Dayton, Ohio, facility, where he did support for the Manhattan program. One of these entailed supporting the raid on Tokyo by Lieutenant Colonel "Jimmy" Doolittle, US Army Air Force, launched from the aircraft carrier USS Hornet on April 18, 1942, one of six US Navy aircraft carrier raids that were launched against Japan in the first half of 1942. After much research and consideration of the complex operational issues the B-25B Mitchell medium bomber was selected for the United States first attack on Japanese soil. With a crew of five the B-25B faced formidable odds both launching from the Hornet yet alone surviving the raid over Tokyo. The B-25B would have no fighter escorts. One key technical issue was would the aircraft with a full weapon load be able to take off from the flight deck of the USS Hornet, given that each aircraft needed a large fuel load to reach the target and then hopefully survive to land at bases in China. If they could not reach these Chinese bases the crews faced the options of either bailing out over eastern China or crash landing along the Chinese coast. In the event of the 16 crews involved 15 aircraft reached the Chinese coast after 13 hours of flight and crashed landed or the crews bailed out. !4 B25Bs crews eventually returned to the United States or reached the safety of American forces. One aircrew was killed while baling out. Eight brave US airmen were captured by the Japanese in eastern China, the other two members of the crews having drowned in the sea. Three of these courageous men were later executed by the Japanese. All but one of the B-25Bs was destroyed in crashes, while the 16th landed at Vladivostok in the Soviet Union. Many variables were involved, not least the wind speed over the deck at the time of launch. The carrier would be faced into the wind to ensure maximum lift. The aerodynamics of Mitchell's B-25B medium bomber came into play. Riley's knowledge, skills, and creative innovation came into play to contribute to the team effort. The young Riley helped ensure that all the aerodynamic and environmental factors were considered and calculated to provide a safe and successful lunch. All up launch weight was clearly a major factor and the equipment inventory of the B-25B was carefully analyzed to determine which pieces of equipment could be sacrificed to reduce all up launch weight. The rest is history. The "Go-Ahead" was given. The facility at Dayton would become a major hub for later US Air Force research and development together with highly specialist classified intelligence and threat assessment programs. Claude Riley's work would encompass from 1947 onwards the theoretical analysis of propulsion systems, the preliminary design of guided missiles, supersonic aerodynamics, flight test of advanced aircraft systems, and the critical development of rocket research technology. All this work had one clear aim, to maintain the technical superiority of the United States and its Allies in a highly charged post World War Two era that would be known as the Cold War, ending with the demise of the Soviet Union (the USSR – the Union of Soviet Socialist Republics), the break up of the Warsaw Pact alliance and the creation in Europe of multiple democratic states that were erstwhile under the tutelage of the Soviet Union.

In 1991 Peace broke out. There were interruptions to this Peace, though not on a global scale. The Balkans conflicts of the 1990s (The Slovenian and Croatian Wars of Independence, the Bosnian War, and the Kosovo Insurgency) disturbed this Peace. Generally the world experienced a new breath of fresh air after decades of the Cold War. This lasted until the terrible events of 911 in 2001 with the attack on the United States, and the demand for new and innovative ways to counter terrorism. Looking back on the world of Claude Riley and the thousands of other fine US scientists and technologists that emerged from World War Two one question arises that was posed by a fine President of the United States in the 1950s, Dwight David Eisenhower (October 14, 1890-March 28, 1969). The latter had indeed both done and seen it all by the time he swore the oath of office as the 34th President of the United States, serving from 1953 to 1961. As the Supreme Commander of the Allied Expeditionary Force in Europe and achieving the five-star rank of General of the Army Dwight Eisenhower had a unique and indeed very perceptive view of the world and the role of war. He coined a phrase that resonated throughout the United States and beyond, reflecting a concern that he had as he watched the way the world was moving in the post World War Two era. He talked explicitly of the "Industrial-Military Complex". He was issuing a warning. He was an advocate for NATO and supporting US Allies, and his main goals in office were to contain the spread of communism and reduce federal deficits. He wanted to rely heavily on nuclear deterrence and also recognized Taiwan as the legitimate government of China, continuing the policy of his predecessor, Harry S. Truman. He condemned the Israeli, British, and French invasion of Egypt in 1956 and forced them to withdraw, and he condemned the Soviet invasion of Hungary during the 1956 Soviet invasion of Hungary. He did approve the Bay of Pigs invasion that was left to his successor, John F. Kennedy, to carry out. As a moderate Conservative Eisenhower continued New Deal agencies, expanded Social Security, and opposed Senator Joseph McCarthy and contributed to the end of McCarthyism by invoking executive privilege. He signed the Civil Rights Act of 1957. and ordered the integration of schools in Little Rock, Arkansas. He led the development and construction of the Interstate Highway System which remains the largest construction of roadways in American history. Apropos the work of Claude Riley and millions of other Americans his two term presidency saw unprecedented economic prosperity except for a minor recession in 1958. In his final farewell address to the American people he gave voice to his concerns about the dangers of massive military spending, particularly if it leads to deficit spending. He stated concerns about huge contracts to contractors supporting the US military, which he dubbed "The Military-Industrial Complex". Stepping back all these decades later it is perhaps beneficial to assess where the post World War Two heavy investment in military technology led. This is important because it is linked to a critical factor, and the theme of this book, the pursuit and preservation of peace. Two very significant events may help shed light on what happened to the United States in the early post World War Two years and that led to the US becoming the preeminent technological leader in the World ... Two "Projects" were created by the US government, lost now in time yet critical to why the United States became the leader of the Free World and a technological giant.

These Projects were "Project Overcast" and "Project Paperclip". In essence both projects were related to how the United States took the very best brains from Nazi Germany, brought them to the United States, and converted their significant brainpower to the service of peace and freedom.

Claude Riley, with many others, was intimately involved in developing new and innovative US systems and technologies, working side-by-side with previous Nazi technical leaders. The leader of this outstanding group of new US citizens from the United States' earlier deadly opponent was Werner von Braun. The latter changed the face of American key technologies and provided the basis for multiple new programs that were in the service of both national defense and the commercial sector. The latter was hugely invigorated by the impact of their scientific and technical contributions, bringing new ideas and innovations that quickly took the United States to the forefront in multiple domains, which created new industries, companies, millions of American jobs, and significant wealth. The commercial impact and benefits for US society and the world were huge. Ram jets figured early in these multiple developments, together with today programs long forgotten though hugely significant in the development of many commercial technologies. The GAM-63 RASCAL supersonic air-to-service missile developed by the Bell

Aircraft Company gave the US Air Force a significant lead. Von Braun's work and leadership provided the technical means for the development of the Saturn 2 rocket and the ability for the US to put a man on the moon in 1969. Claude Riley so enjoyed working directly with Werner von Braun and innovating. He owed much to that key introduction to the US Army by a great American, Carl Vinson (1883-1981). Out of this sprang Claude Riley's work on supersonic aircraft and the first manned aircraft to break the sound barrier, all stemming from Riley's initial key work at Dayton producing polonium for the Manhattan Program at Los Alamos. Polonium was the critical material that early in 1943 radio chemists at Los Alamos found was the best initiator for the gun assembly component within the system. Dayton played a crucial role in producing the all important initiator for the Manhattan Project. Claude Riley was part of the team, cutting his technical teeth on a war ending system that also changed the world and the future of mankind. Beyond Dayton Claude Riley's work with Wernher von Braun, "The Father of Rocket Science and Space Exploration", helped ensure the long term success of American systems and technologies. Claude Riley's brilliant work continued until the end of the 20th century and retirement. He worked on a large number of highly classified US government programs. With thousands of others he made a difference. It is important to consider and evaluate President Eisenhower's closing Address to the American people in the context of what we now know, from the vantage point and perspective of 2024. The world has mercifully avoided the worst cataclysm of a nuclear exchange. However, we live in an era of violence precipitated by the February, 2022 Russian invasion of Ukraine and the October 7, 2023 attack on Israel by Hamas and the subsequent counter attack by Israel on Palestinian Gaza. Vladimir Putin has torn up decades of successful nuclear control mechanisms between the United States and first the Soviet Union, then Russia. No nuclear weapons agreements currently exist between the United States and Russia to both control nuclear weapons numbers and production and, equally if not more important, control mechanisms and communications to avoid worst case nuclear accidents and events. The above places ever more need for advanced technologies to support the US and Allied nuclear warnings and indicators systems. This applies equally to China and North Korea. The other nuclear powers have reliable control and communications systems – the UK, France, India, Pakistan, and Israel. Proliferation to Iraq will create a whole new set of threat variables.

There may have been "Over Investment" in the Eisenhower era in defense related programs. No one knows with any degree of accuracy. That kind of assessment may be very difficult to conduct without perhaps the most capable analytics of data that is old, and perhaps not even available. However, one key aspect emerges. The life and work of Claude Riley, and thousands of Americans like him, created the current United States industrial lead, whatever is currently stated about the challenges from China. Science and the technological developments from it have provided the US economy and people with a massive lead across all defense and commercial applications. There are serious rivals, of course, India and China perhaps leading the rivals to American technical preeminence. However, US innovation is still at its finest.

The wars in Korea, Vietnam, Iraq, and Afghanistan, together with numerous interventions and other military operations, such as the Balkans and Libya for examples, have had serious consequences for global peace. They were, perhaps, in certain cases, not all, the result of strategic error on the part of the US leadership. The invasion of Iraq clearly bears examination under this rubric. However, one key thing we do know is this. Science has not been the cause of conflict. It has clearly and inevitably been a crucial factor. No question. This self evident fact belies one very crucial observation. Science has been and is a very crucial factor in the preservation of peace. Why is this? Without advances in science and the conversion to critical systems and technologies the United States and its Allies may not have been able to achieve victory in the greatest war in the history of mankind, and to avoid to date a major confrontation of the worst kind between global powers. The nature of man and the leadership of the world's nations have sadly demonstrated that the lessons of war have not been learned and implanted in the cultures, hearts and minds of nations whose leaders do not follow the great democratic traditions of the United States and its key allies. The future is what we all make it. At the national level it is what our elected leadership decides and does. Science will continue to play a crucial role in the preservation of peace. Many challenges lie ahead.

THREE

SCIENCE AND PEACE – THE CONTINUUM

In an Age of rapid Technical Change: People & Innovation

The world events since September 11, 2011 have shaken the resolve of many nations, particularly within NATO, where member nations have witnessed and become somewhat disenchanted with out -of-area operations and commitments to operations that have gone sadly and strategically out of kilter. Iraq, Afghanistan and Libya come immediately to mind, and each of these emphasize above all, the lack of wide-ranging strategic thinking not just about the how and what, but the why. For example, vast cultural differences and huge sectarian rifts that have spanned the centuries within the Moslem world, with their critical ethnic, religious and regional affinities, were largely ignored in a somewhat heedless and headlong dash to seek reprisal for the events of 9/11, for what initially was a small terrorist organization, manned largely by Saudi nationals, not Iraqis or Iranians, with limited funds and resources. Lessons learned from the past, if applied judiciously, may prove invaluable in the preservation of peace. One aspect seems crucial: Intelligence. The combined strength of Five Eyes intelligence has to be a formidable instrument of strategic power in the service of the security of the collective nations. This predicates the need for a "Shared Five Eyes Intelligence Vision." Intelligence is only valuable to the user if is superior to normal open-source information, and that provides both clear benefits for decision makers and advantages in terms of insight into and knowledge of the particular subject matter. Ultimately the "game of intelligence," as played out for instance during the Cold War by the various HUMINT services of the main international protagonists, is not relevant unless there is real hard-core information emanating from that process. Pitting one secret intelligence service against another may be the subject of spy fiction but it is irrelevant to the essence of providing actionable, accurate, and timely classified information of real value. The pace and quality of technological change has accelerated drastically in the last decade. US-UK Intelligence and the Five Eyes governments have tended to be behind the curve in responding to technological change, with outmoded contracting systems and timelines from R&D phases to initial operational capability (IOC) woefully slow and ponderous, with the result that the commercial, non-defense intelligence world is far more ahead of the technical game because of the ability to innovate quickly and effectively. All this is in contrast to what was described and discussed in the challenge to peace during and in the years after World War Two. Small start-up incubator companies have become the name of the commercial game not just in Silicon Valley but across the whole Five Eyes industrial and scientific base. Five Eyes governments have tried to step up the pace, but have not succeeded to date, with post-DARPA-esque organizations such as the United States DIU (Defense Innovation Unit) failing to deliver for a host of bureaucratic, funding, and political reasons. We noted earlier that large defense and aerospace companies with massive multi-year contracts that seriously influence their bottom lines and annual shareholder returns are chastened by the possibility of small start-ups that can well negate the value of the very programs that are their financial life blood. This aspect is a problem that has to be addressed. All the above is in start contrast with what was observed and discussed about the Eisenhower era and how Claude Riley and his thousands of able contemporaries made things happen. There are solutions for all parties. For example, the more systems of whatever technical nature are open architecture, with the ability to introduce major innovative changes without starting from scratch. In this environment radical innovations can be quickly implemented without the costly multi-year cycle of typical procurements within the defense and intelligence sectors. Intelligence has a massive technical component.

All US-UK Intelligence and Five Eyes key agencies that both cost most in annual budgets and employ most people are at the leading edge of technology. They live and breathe, and one may conjecture possibly die in the future, by being one or more steps ahead technologically than the threat. To fall behind is to fail. At the heart of this issue is, simply, people, and very smart people. US-UK Intelligence will have to increasingly search for, recruit, and train the next generation, and most of all allow for innovation to occur at the grass roots, just as the pressures and exigencies of war and survival forced the British to recruit the finest minds to Bletchley Park, SOE, and the Double Cross system. Across the Five Eyes community there will need to be a "Brains Trust" of the best and the brightest to keep the community ahead. Greater cooperation and sharing will become more critical within closely guarded compartmented programs, very much along the lines of the US Navy–Royal Navy special intelligence collection and analysis programs. The non-military customers' requirements of the Five Eyes may on the surface look very different from those of the military services but on close inspection there is in fact considerable similarity and overlap, where in the 21st century the digital communications revolution affects for instance foreign policy decision making that overlap with understanding and countering threat weapon systems. The intelligence products, and uses to which they are put, may be different but the essence of the collection sources, methods, and analysis may be very similar in an increasingly artificial intelligence-oriented world in which data sources bear no resemblance to the days of the Cold War. This will require a restructuring of US-UK Intelligence and the Five Eyes intelligence education and training, requiring experts with proven successful track records to design and implement courses that inspire innovation. US-UK Intelligence in 2024 is now in a "Brave New World of Next Generation Technologies". The "5G" international technical race has been running for some time. The companies that will win this race will have unprecedented commercial power, and therefore from an intelligence perspective it is critical that both the US and the UK and their Five Eyes partners are 100 per cent not just well informed but also planning how they will interact with what will be a further revolution in global telecommunications. For those not well versed in telecommunications you may ask what is 5G and what will be its impact? 5G is a disruptive technology that will make current use of our cell phones and other digital telecommunications devices look like dinosaurs, because they will in fact be dinosaurs. They will be the fifth generation of systems. 5G devices will be at least one hundred times faster than what you have today in 2020. They will use ultra-low energy, will have extreme broadband (your data rates will boggle the mind), high reliability, flawless mobility (where and when you use), with ultra-low latency, and deep coverage globally and, most of all, low cost. Latency is where battery life is extended without affecting performance, and data is processed at much higher rates. There is therefore a technical challenge to achieve increased processing power while conserving energy. Whoever comes out on top in this race will have a huge commercial gain. From an intelligence perspective understanding and knowing the technical complexities, and exploitation of 5G systems and the global telecommunications architectures that will support it is paramount. It will require the best of the best in technical intelligence know-how to exploit. Who then are the key players? They may be divided for convenience sake into "Big Boys" and "Little Boys." The former are the top telecommunications carriers and manufacturers: Huawei, ZTE, Ericsson, Nokia, and Samsung. The latter are: Deutsche Telecom, Sprint, Orange, SK Telecom, Korea Telecom, T-Mobile, AT&T, Verizon, and US Cellular. There may be others that join the race in due course. It is a strategic imperative that the Five Eyes anticipate every technical dimension of this race and who does what, where, and how. The exploitation strategy must be designed and implemented well in advance of these systems and the telecommunications architectures of the main players reaching the global marketplace. The question of what the next generation after 5G will look like, is a strategic issue for US-UK Intelligence and the Five Eyes to address, anticipate, and plan for. One of the characteristics of Five Eyes intelligence and procurement systems has been the linear extrapolation of technology, rather than innovative step changes. The natural business cycle between Five Eyes contractors and their government agencies has been to improve on the last system. This makes absolute sense at one level. If you can make an intelligence collection system or an analytical tool better than this makes absolute sense. The downside is that the whole technical and procurement system tends towards conservative change. DARPA in the US has a history to a certain extent of avoiding this pitfall and supporting leading edge, even over the top high risk, innovation. However, even DARPA programs have life spans that are extraordinarily lengthy before they eventually transition to a real-world application, so that in many cases they are no longer innovative and may indeed be costly dinosaurs. I worked on one highly classified DARPA program that was years in the gestation and although its output was technically innovative, by the time it could be integrated as an operational system it had lost its edge and was excessively costly. The science behind it was outstanding, but the US government simply could not convert to an operational system in the right timeline. Winston Churchill had a simple phrase when he issued a direct order saying make something happen immediately: "Action This Day!" It may seem antiquated to reinvent this particular Churchillian aphorism, but on close inspection it really is not. Catastrophic cyber-attacks will require in the coming decades the same degree of instant action, anticipating and mitigating the threats by well-prepared and rapidly implemented counterstrokes. The latter is what may be termed the "Golden Eggs" syndrome. In other words, for the Five Eyes to have in their intelligence basket a whole collection of golden eggs that have not just anticipated the threats' challenges but have at the ready effective means to counter and deceptively negate the enemy's capabilities by highly secure covert means. This resilience is essential for US-UK Intelligence and the Five Eyes in the coming generation. It will take cooperation and the willingness to share intellectual property in the most secure ways. The vetting of participants must be rigorous and new security systems to obviate the worst kind of internal treachery must be in place. The latter requires a whole new systems and technology base. For example, if another Edward Snowden began to interrogate highly classified data and then download to thumb drives, new systems would not only immediately alert, track, and interrogate such actions, but also prevent access in the first place by the most rigorous AI applications. If system denial comes up on the screen, then the user will have to justify access to a superior. We know that the ocean floor in 2016 had about 300 major transoceanic submarine cables carrying approximately $4 trillion worth of banking, commercial and personal transactions of one sort or another, in addition to about 95% oM the world's voice and internet traffic.1 In 2020 these numbers have increase exponentially and from an intelligence perspective, 95% of the world's key dat and communications pass through undersea fiber-optic cables. An examination o who laid these cables, who owns them, who operates and maintains them clearl raises key questions about their intelligence value. Shades of Blinker Hall? Well yes, is the simple answer. Much of the data, voice, and imagery will be heavil encrypted and passing in discreet transmission modes. In those cables, together wit space-based communications systems, landline systems, and microwave tower-base transmissions lay intelligence nuggets. The sheer volume of traffic alone is a great technical challenge for Five Eyes intelligence. It will require the most sophisticated AI tools to interrogate such data, provided the Five Eyes can collectively retrieve data in a timely manner. If we re-examine how quickly and efficiently Blinker Hall's team intercepted and decrypted the Zimmermann Telegram and then compare the similar tasks of the 2020s and beyond it will be appreciated just how things have changed and the intellectual challenge ahead. The good news is that what human beings invent, design, engineer, and implement can likewise be understood and countered. The inventiveness and intellectual prowess of the Five Eyes will have to be married to new forms of deception and technical artfulness that is sustained by highly resilient systems. Internally US-UK Intelligence and the Five Eyes as a whole will require more and more back-ups, and across-the-board power sources and power distribution protection, communications resiliency, discreet standalone cyber detection systems, and ways to mitigate threat access by clever use of new electronic deception tools. Classical Cold War electronic jamming will seem old hat compared to the demands of ensuring GPS systems and transmissions survivability and durability as the 2020s pass into the 2030s. Surprises are never welcome in the Five Eyes intelligence community, whether it is warnings and indicators against, for example, a Chinese surprise attack against Taiwan, or new and insidious ways for threat nations and their surrogates to undermine the Five Eyes and their allies and friendly nations in maintaining critical infrastructure and, in the case of the military, the resupply and transport of military personnel and equipment in a timely and effective way to threat areas. The worst-case technological surprise scenario is likely to come from the realm of quantum resistant cryptography, a domain in which US-UK Intelligence and the Five Eyes must pool their brain power and resources to avoid a bombshell like impact on communications, security, and the ability of the Five Eyes to remain electronically dominant. Encryption is vital for US-UK Intelligence and the Five Eyes for internal security and, conversely, the ability to break others encryption is the other side of the coin. There is a current concern that high-capacity quantum computers will be able to break the most sophisticated current encryptions, presenting unacceptable vulnerabilities from a Five Eyes perspective. The current sophisticated human-created algorithms that supposedly are randomly generated numbers, but in fact are not, will be solvable by quantum computers.

The latter are a step change in technology, using photons, neutrons, protons, and electrons to execute hugely sophisticated calculations versus ones and zeros. Quantum computers will be the new super computers of the 2030s and beyond. US-UK Intelligence must ensure that this critical pillar of information security, encryption, is both not undermined and at the same time a lead must be made in striking out technically against adversaries using that very capability. The goal will be for the Five Eyes as a whole to create mutual technology that will be "Quantum Resistant" while exploiting thecapability to decrypt others' transmissions. New forms of technical deception can provide bulwarks against invasive attacks on all forms of civilian, military, political, and commercial infrastructure and operations. The great strength of the Five Eyes is the natural distribution of its many and varied global intelligence assets. Sharing data has to be top of the list, underscored by personnel exchanges, and with highly compartmented security arrangements. The most significant differentiator of the 2020s from the post-World War II era is that the civilian world in peacetime is as equally vulnerable to a wide range of electronic attack that was not technically possible earlier. Individuals, banks, the international financial structure, transport, and all other forms of critical infrastructure from power and water supply to communications and the media are subject to state-sponsored cyber-attacks, and those of state-sponsored surrogates, criminal organizations, and malicious hackers. Next generation technologies have to be not only anticipated and worked on in terms of basic R&D by the collective Five Eyes, they have to be ahead in both capability and timescale of not just current threats but those predicted over the next ten to twenty years. US-UK Intelligence and the Five Eyes are challenged in both the civilian and military sectors. These encompass anti-access, area denial weapons and non-kinetic systems, cyber warfare and the wider electronic warfare spectrum, together with what are now a vast range of information threats, and a range of asymmetric threats. The latter cover not just the Five Eyes military but their civilian populations and those of their allies and friendly nations with whom they trade. ISIS is not at all dead. It is proliferating in Africa and Asia in unprecedented ways. In themselves the advanced technologies under review, such as big data analytics, artificial intelligence, autonomous systems, robotics, directed energy, hypersonic, biotechnology, and advanced space and airborne surveillance systems and sensors (including drones, UAVs, and UCASs), are not enough. US-UK Intelligence and the Five Eyes will have to integrate these technologies into tactical and strategic operational systems across the breadth and depth of all Five Eyes countries in the most highly secure and compartmented ways with internal threat security systems of the highest order. In this process one aspect is uppermost. Cooperation is essential. No one country can monopolize crucial technology. We witnessed how intelligence sharing in World War II helped save the day. To support these developments the Five Eyes will have to develop together the necessary planning and training for joint implementation. The bottom line is that these developments must be shown to impact decision-making to justify overall Five Eyes intelligence investment. Education within the Five Eyes intelligence community is critical, with both the scientific and technical intelligence directorates working alongside operational intelligence personnel, to ensure that not just the most effective programs are pursued but also that training courses are designed on an across-the-board basis so that American, British, Canadian, Australian, and New Zealand personnel share training under a common umbrella. We know from past experience that the camaraderie and cross fertilization of ideas between the nations' intelligence communities yield huge dividends. It is recommended that civilians and military personnel are mixed so that there is mutual exposure to threats, needs, and solutions, together with the incubation of new tradecraft, sources, methods, and analysis. The Five Eyes can collectively develop from this process new intelligence doctrine and operational plans, and commit these to policy agreements as add-ons to existing agreements, and kept highly secure. The above is predicated, as always, on good visionary leadership. Historically, the lead nation in terms of investment and global sources and methods has been the United States. However, for the above to be successful the United States will have to be open and sharing within strict compartmented intelligence parameters. In parallel each of the Five Eyes' military schools and war colleges should be drawn into this process, both in terms of inputs and also training and education. There has to be more dialogue between these five communities. Intelligence training schools and the war colleges need more synergism. We have learned since World War II that nothing encourages this more than personnel exchange programs, so that not just ideas and information are exchanged and developed but most of all personal relationships are developed that can be bedrock for the rest of people's careers. The benefits in a crisis are legion. I remember well at the height of the Cold War regularly picking up the secure phone and calling my opposite numbers in each of the Five Eyes nations and almost daily on some occasions leaving my office to visit various intelligence personnel in either the London embassies or in various UK exchange locations. We never, ever, failed and, in the words of Admiral William McRaven, formerly Commander of Naval Special Warfare and Commander of Special Operations Command, spoken at the University of Texas Class of 2014 Commencement Ceremony in June 2014, "We never, ever, rang the Bell!" We stood together in the spirit of US-UK Intelligence and Five Eyes cooperation and although at times we may not always have agreed on whatever, we never stopped working together in the spirit of total committed cooperation. Russia has used social media disinformation to attack the western media and sow doubt and dissension amongst all levels of society from intellectual elites to the less educated. This divisiveness strategy is difficult to measure in terms of overall effects, but the intelligence objectives are clear cut, namely, to create political and social divisions within and between the key democracies. Disinformation is a formidable weapon in the deception armory. Scare tactics using false information confuse and dissemble otherwise stable and fair-minded people. The Kremlin has directly driven these tactics. Its goals are to shape public opinion over a wide range of events, issues, and policies. These include, for examples, the 2016 US election, BREXIT, the

Khashoggi murder, the downing with Russian missiles of flight MH-17, the poisoning of the Skripals in Salisbury, England, chemical attacks by the Assad regime in Syria, Russia's de facto invasions of eastern Ukraine and the illegal annexation of the Crimea, and many other social media disinformation campaigns. The Five Eyes has extraordinary talent to not just counter these attacks but turn them around against the Russian regime. US-UK Intelligence and the Five Eyes have enormous potential capabilities to counter using, for one unclassified example, AI. The opposition will use AI as much as the Five Eyes. The latter have to be many steps ahead, all the time. Project Maven in the US was under contract in two months and a capability was delivered in six months.2 Maven (also known as Algorithmic Warfare Cross Functional Team) uses advanced secure AI algorithms to analyze in real-time key data from multiple sources and methods. Vladimir Putin fully understands AI's value. Speaking in 2017 he said, "It comes with colossal opportunities, but also threats that are difficult to predict. Whoever becomes the leader in this sphere will become the ruler of the world."3 US-UK Intelligence and the Five Eyes need to be way ahead all the time as Putin's Foundation for Advanced Studies (a DARPA-like equivalent) seeks equivalency and terrorists use social network mapping, AI-enabled drones, and social engineering attacks to both recruit and undermine stable populations. Counterterrorism intelligence within the UK–US and wider Five Eyes community will need to concentrate joint resources in identifying in real time and eliminating from the worldwide web such terrorist material. Radicalization and extremism are growing, not diminishing. US-UK Intelligence and the Five Eyes will have to collectively extend current public–private technical partnerships to stay ahead of the threat and undermine it before it has effect. Similarly, with international hostage taking and kidnapping, where UK–US intelligence can use AI-based systems and technology to detect, locate, track, and eliminate criminal and politically inspired hostage and kidnap entities. On the military side it will be possible using AI-based technologies with various discreet advanced sensors and guidance systems to use lethal autonomous weapons by the Five Eyes nations and their key allies in real-time situations against terrorist targets, in ways that were impossible with earlier systems like Hellfire missiles on various UAVs, such as Reaper and Global Hawk. The ability to process massive amounts of discreet intelligence data and make accurate real-time decisions beyond normal human operating speeds will change the rules of the game in the counterterrorist fight. The US National Cyber Strategy and the US Defense Department's Cyber Strategy released in September 2018, call for defense of the homeland, to protect American prosperity, deter, detect and punish malicious actors, and with allies push for an "open, interoperable, reliable, and secure internet," and also protecting US space assets simultaneously. Russia and China are clearly identified as adversaries, with China "eroding US military overmatch and is persistently exfiltrating sensitive information from the US public and private sector." In a contested public, private, and military–political cyberspace environment the Five Eyes clearly need to be not just one step ahead but many, so that high-level policy documents such as the one quoted above have real flesh on the bones of what are somewhat obvious goals to even the less knowledgeable layperson. Five Eyes collaboration is paramount. The US cannot go it alone and most pleasingly the Pentagon has stated its objective to "strengthen the capacity of allies and partners and increase DOD's ability to leverage its partners' unique skills, resources, capabilities, and perspectives." At one level this may be seen by the Five Eyes community as US patronage. However, given the strong historic bonds the younger generation in the US Department of Defense, with little or no knowledge of the Five Eyes' historic record, will need to be both educated and inducted into the Five Eyes community. One key solution lies in the huge historic bedrock experience of UK–US Intelligence in deception. Deception helped win World War II and certainly shortened it, and in the assessment made by Sir Harry Hinsley, the official historian of British intelligence in World War II, may have shortened the war with the combined strengths of ENIGMA and the MAGIC by as much as two years. Cyberspace offers myriad ways for the Five Eyes to cooperatively outthink, outmaneuver, and overwhelm both peer level threats and also low-level terrorist groups and criminal hackers and their paymasters. Classification naturally prohibits disclosure. Suffice to say that the US and the UK together with the other three Five Eyes nations have enormous resources and intellectual pedigree to outflank any of the threats referenced earlier. Reaching a major conflict zone, staying there successfully and accomplishing various missions, is now not as easy as it was even ten years ago in 2010. To sustain persistent forward presence say in the Pacific and particularly the South China Sea and adjacent sea areas, the US has the weapons and overall force structure to accomplish various missions laid down in national strategic plans in the event of various threat scenarios. However, intelligence shows that peer military adversaries could attempt to block, interrupt, and worst case kinetically challenge US presence and intervention. In this increasingly complex environment Deception, with a very big "D," becomes essential. The threat must never know what it doesn't know and be made to believe a whole host of conflicting informational aspects, while denied, deceived, and disrupted by the most subtle and egregious means. The threat must have zero knowledge of what the Five Eyes are both doing, and could expand as situations deteriorate. Various silver bullets need to be preserved for the ultimate threats, kept under the most secure wraps until needed. Winston Churchill and Franklin Roosevelt, and their key top military commanders, are excellent role models in this regard. They preserved and protected their most secret deception plans and technologies, and only employed them when the timing was just right. The Five Eyes have the brains, the technology, the cultural and social adhesiveness, plus the binding agreements of decades, to work against several adversaries who have nothing like the cohesiveness of the Five Eyes. In parallel to the big "D" are other technological advances, from robotic operating systems on the land, the sea surface, underwater, and in the air, with unmanned systems, embedded and mobile sensors enhanced by onboard data processing systems, with AI dominant, so that operators are assisted in decision making functions, rather than being overwhelmed by saturated information. The Five Eyes can empower commanders with critical decision-making information, coupled with advances in AI-focused space-based systems that provide resiliency in contested environments so that Five Eyes space-based communications remain secure and intact. All the above will need integration with planned advances in high energy lasers, hypersonic vehicles and weapons, and the hypersonic propulsion systems that carry them. In due course the Five Eyes will have the ability to challenge most threats in ways that were inconceivable less than a decade ago. The problems that have been very eruditely analyzed by Jonathan Ward in his paper, "Sino-Indian Competition in the Maritime Domain"4 may hopefully not come to pass if all the above becomes increasingly clear to peer competitors, as a major deterrent to aggressive action that may precipitate crisis. The wise words of former US Navy Secretary Richard Danzig may indeed come to pass, that "promoting innovation and enhancing lethality should become a higher priority than acquiring additional ships."5 *Time* magazine in its June 4, 2018 edition discussed with and analyzed various intelligence related aspects with then Director of National Intelligence Dan Coats. The article indicated that Director Coats, with a background on the US Senate Select Intelligence Committee, and Ambassador to Germany 2001–2005, has solid credentials, but caveated that he may not be able to convince his President of the value of the US intelligence community's intelligence assessments over issues, for example, relating to Iranian nuclear weapon development compliance. In this environment US-UK Intelligence becomes ever more critical as a collective mouthpiece of intelligence credibility, standing firm on well-reasoned analysis based on thorough and accurate sources and methods. In this context US-UK Intelligence and its political oversight and leadership assume a new dimensional role. This became self-evident in the August 2019 with the resignation of Director Coats, followed shortly afterwards by his Principal Deputy Director, Susan M. Gordon, emphasizing that good unvarnished non-politically-oriented intelligence can only serve the national interest if there is independence from political influence, a hugely different concept from political oversight. What has evolved from the above discussion is the need for an overall Five Eyes "Grand Strategy" based on one key notion that intelligence is a dynamic living process and is never static. A biannual "summit" of all the key players from all the Five Eyes intelligence departments and agencies could take place rotationally in each of the five capitals. During the intervening two years working groups and round tables from the many and varied specialist intelligence communities can work on the issues of the day and those predicted in the future, and deliver the most important issues for resolution at the summit. Regularity of meetings is essential in an era when the nature of all the threats that we have addressed, and many than none of us can ever foresee or anticipate, demands meetings of the minds. Such summits can agree on threats, consolidate solutions, initiate joint technology and operational cooperation, with the necessary planning and budgets. The summit members can have their best national advisors present, with one key objective of agreeing on the next phase in the technological revolution and its impact on intelligence collection and analysis. From a security perspective the Five Eyes summit will need to compartmentalize special programs and lay down security guidelines. In the wider security context, it is important that the Five Eyes have agreed ways to uniformly address the insider threat, to mitigate the worst of internal treachery. The Five Eyes should not be hesitant in sharing systems and technology that undermine those who betray the Five Eyes internally. Given good compartmentalization it does not follow that one bad apple will ruin the whole barrel, but nonetheless one bad apple can create enormous damage. We saw historically what Philby did in the UK and the Walkers in the US. One increasingly strategic issue that such summits must face is the civilian–commercial world interface with government. Cyber threats to every level of society and activity, and attacks on critical commercial intellectual property and defense and security technology require new approaches to educating and training the Five Eyes public and businesses in countering these pervasive threats. Exfiltration of intellectual property is a massive economic and security threat. This applies to not just cyber threats but also physical and personnel security. Part of the summit process will likely be a domain that is neglected at least from the public's perspective. This is economic intelligence. We tend to concentrate so much on all the other "INTs" and the many threats that confront us that we can easily forget many of the global economic issues that may well be transformed into threat scenarios. Most are aware of the impact of oil and gas issues that have driven foreign and commercial policies for decades and how protection of oil and gas flow to the economies of the democracies has been paramount. None of this will change. However other equally pervasive economic issues may constitute compelling threats in the future. Water rights and water supply issues may become more and more serious. An analysis of all the critical minerals that make up electronic components and whole systems, such as vehicles and aircraft, let alone domestic products, reveals the delicate international economic balance regarding which countries have which minerals and their commercial destinations. In the 21st century the global economic heartland may well be predicated on what minerals are needed for which industries and products and their location and supply chain. For these summits to be successful and indeed for the whole Five Eyes community to be successful for the foreseeable future, we must have a clear and well-articulated statement of what "Five Eyes Strategy" is. Grand intelligence strategy is not about "how" and "what" all these various entities do and their fine products. It is, very simply, "why" they do what they do at any moment in time. The "what" and "how" come later, as implementation. There is one overriding element that determines the "why." *These are the vital national interests of each of the Five Eyes, and their combined collective interests. These interests drive the "Why." They drive the Five Eyes intelligence community machinery that will provide the vital security for modern society now and for the foreseeable future.* Without clear definitions of what are these vital national interests, and indeed these will change over time as the global situation changes in its many and varied forms, the great historic intelligence traditions of US-UK Intelligence and the Five Eyes as a whole will be grasping at straws. On August 10, 1941 Winston Churchill and Franklin Roosevelt met on board HMS *Prince of Wales* in Placentia Bay, off Newfoundland. The President had sailed from Washington DC in USS *Augusta*. At that meeting these two great men agreed one fundamental thing, grand strategy to defeat Nazism, and this strategy was predicated on one key basic tenet, the vital national interests of the United Kingdom and the United States. The Five Eyes will have to continuously address the changing global scene and adjust their intelligence operations, technology, sources, methods, and analysis to those vital national interests defined by their political leadership.

The history of US-UK Intelligence is an incredible history of cooperation and dedication. The heart and soul of US-UK Intelligence is at the working level, the intelligence specialists from the United States, the United Kingdom, Canada, Australia, and New Zealand that have greatly served this extraordinary community. They have and will continue to serve with great distinction. I have been hugely privileged over a 50-year period to have participated in this great community, my roles minuscule as they were in the truly great scheme of things, but like all of us who lived and worked in this community during this turbulent and challenging 50 years, the sum of all the efforts, dedication, hard work, and sacrifice of everyone made a massive difference. I really believe that this international intelligence community reflects and represents the core strengths and values of these five great democracies, epitomizing the ability of each and every country to stay the course, not to waiver, and be steadfastly consistent and loyal in the darkest hours as well as the bright moments of triumph. The essence of US-UK Intelligence and the Five Eyes as a whole is an "Enduring Culture". What occurred within US-UK Intelligence that was conveyed to the Five Eyes community as a whole, in retrospect, is quite remarkable. Governments for the past 79 years since 1945 have come and gone, but US-UK Intelligence and the Five Eyes have survived without any serious threat to their existence. There have been challenges, but on the whole the abiding professional loyalty that has bound the large number of individuals together, past and present, is emblematic of something much deeper and more sustainable than political change. At one level the Five Eyes have defined the strength of the values and commitment that underpin the essence of each nation's sense of democracy and freedom in a very uncertain world. There have been political variances within the Five Eyes political hierarchies over issues associated with, for example, the Suez campaign by the British and the war in Vietnam by the United States, but none of these issues have ever undermined the bedrock relationships. The Five Eyes stood together when North Korea invaded South Korea on June 25, 1950, and fought alongside each other, sharing intelligence, until the war ended on July 27, 1953 with an armistice agreement. The UK fought a successful counterinsurgency campaign in Malaysia and received maximum support from its Commonwealth Five Eyes members. The British supported the US clandestinely in East Asia during the Vietnam War, and the US came headlong in support of the British in the 1982 Falklands campaign. Whatever the political differences over the Middle East foreign policies of the US and Britain, with the other three nations tending to play out their international political roles via the United Nations, the intelligence process based on the core relationships at the working level has endured.

The future of US-UK Intelligence and the Five Eyes as a whole is in the hands of a new generation that will continue the great work and traditions of the past. The bonds that will continue to bind them together were created by several generations that began during the dark days of World War Two. They will go on, and they will endure. The Photograph below should remind us all of the bonds created by two great leaders when the world was totally challenged. The pursuit of peace has to be the quintessential motive and role of science in supporting all the innovation discussed above. It is the motivating force that keeps alive the very reasons for all the future needs and requirement of one highly crucial peace keeping domain, Intelligence, and the science that will drive and underpin its future success in maintaining peace.

The Great Tradition that will endure
to ensure the Pursuit of Peace
United States and British Intelligence
Providing abiding Security in an Uncertain
and Challenging World

Winston Churchill, Franklin D. Roosevelt, Admiral Stark, and Admiral King on board HMS *Prince of Wales* in Placentia Bay off Newfoundland, August 10, 1941. The relationships that were established at this momentous meeting have endured for the past 83 years. In the new era the spirit of Franklin Roosevelt and Winston Churchill will live on in a fine new generation of United States and British Intelligence personnel. Let know one threaten this critical relationship as the US and the UK, the Five Eyes as a whole, and their allies face the changes of the 21st century.

This relationship is critical in "The Pursuit of Peace".

FOUR

CLAUDE RILEY EPILOGUE

When Claude Riley passed away in 2012 at age 92 he left behind a huge legacy, distinguished by the many scientific and technical innovations that he made towards the Pursuit of Peace during a lifetime that witnessed war on an enormous and unprecedented scale. His contribution was one of many thousands. However, what his life illustrates is how one human being, man or woman, can make a difference in the unique way that each human being can. All of us can contribute to peace, in whatever way is applicable to our talents and experience, as well as our own motivation, geography, and opportunities presented to each of us uniquely. We do not have to be a Claude Riley, simply just ourselves. What Claude Riley's life and work shows is, very simply at one level, that each individual can make a difference. Claude's passing had one unresolved aspect that should be known. Whether this is related to his long association with Wernher Von Braun (March 23, 1912-June 16, 1977) is not known at this stage. It is important to recall that Claude Riley worked closely with the man who was the leading figure of rocket technology, initially in Nazi Germany, and who became the quintessential lead in United States aerospace engineering and space technology and architecture. He worked on highly classified ballistic missile programs and was the chief architect of the Saturn V super heavy lift launch vehicle that propelled the Apollo spacecraft to the Moon. In 1975 Von Braun was awarded the prestigious National Medal of Science. He advocated a human mission to Mars. His work in Nazi Germany is well documented in multiple open sources. His work in the United States and support at the highest level of the US government, including President Eisenhower who took a direct personal involvement in supporting his work to provide counters to military scientific and technical developments in the Soviet Union. Claude Riley was very much involved in the programs that Von Braun initiated and led. Their families were close. In addition to the work with Von Braun Claude Riley was involved in multiple other sensitive classified programs after Von Braun passed away in 1977. Claude had 35 more years to live. During that time he accomplished many more fine technical achievements for United States' security and the pursuit of peace. Shortly after he died Claude Riley's home was subjected to a serious burglary. The intruders stole only one very specific group of items – all of the documents in his collection of filing cabinets. The extent and nature of these documents is not known. His daughter reported the break-in and thefts to the local police. In due course the Department of Defense was informed and later two Agents from the Naval Criminal Investigation Service (NCIS) visited Claude Riley's home to investigate. They provided their business cards to Riley's daughter. Claude's family never received a report on the investigation, or any subsequent communication from the US government regarding the likely motivation and possible suspects. One can speculate. A significant fact is that the family were informed by the police that no fingerprints were found anywhere on the filing cabinets. Whoever the perpetrators it is likely that there was more than one person given the extent of Riley's filing cabinets' collections. It must surely have been a well planned and secure burglary, carefully orchestrated to ensure zero detection. Two factors clearly come to mind: the motivation and likely suspects. When Claude Riley died his obituaries in the newspapers would have been read by many people, including all the staffs in the multitude of foreign embassies and consulates in Washington DC and around the United States. In addition foreign intelligence services would be following the careers and passing of people of Riley's caliber and significance for US National Security. His open papers were available to the general public, and presentations and papers at open public conferences, including professional associations, would be read as routine by the scientific and technical intelligence communities of those nations not well disposed to the United States, the Five Eyes Intelligence community, and other friendly and allied countries.

The motivation to mount a well conceived theft of Claude Riley's extensive collection of technical papers clearly indicates that the risk was assessed to be worthy given the potential value of the content. It is almost one hundred per cent guaranteed that he would never have retained classified material. So what were the potential benefits?

Within his writings were undoubtedly scientific and technical gold. He had been involved in many critical programs requiring the finest of minds. The core technical ideas and concepts need not have been classified until applied to very specific programs that were indeed classified.

Stealing several cabinets full of his personal papers must have been assessed to be of considerable benefit for whoever was the end user. Such papers could have been associated with other more sensitive foreign sources and methods about US defense programs that would enable a foreign intelligence agency to integrate Claude Riley's personal collection into more broadly based intelligence assessments.

At this stage, in 2024, no further information is available.

The most likely suspects can be surmised. Their motivation and modus operandi in conducting the theft are easy to understand.

So there remains a mystery over the passing of a fine American, great patriot, and public servant who contributed to the "Pursuit of Peace".

FIVE

ANTECEDENTS FOR A YOUNG LAWYER ON THE WORLD WAR TWO BATTLEFIELD

Benjamin (Ben) Ferencz was born in Transylvania, Romania on March 11, 1920. He passed away on April 7, 2023, aged 103. By any standards Ben Ferencz not only lived a long life he lived a remarkable life with a lasting legacy. He was born into a Jewish family. His parents brought him to the United States when he was just ten months old, in 1921. In 1933 Adolf Hitler came to power in Germany and within three short years he took Germany from a democracy under the erstwhile Weimar Republic to not just a dictatorship also a police state. By 1936 the dye was cast in Nazi Germany. A police state controlled the German people with the three Nazi organizations, the Gestapo, Sicherheitsdienst (SD), and Schutzstaffel (SS) watching constantly every move made by any individual, group, or organization that opposed Hitler's policies. Between 1936 and September, 1939 Hitler and his entourage of evil doers eliminated opponents by imprisonment, execution, and murder. On September 3rd 1939 the United Kingdom declared war on Germany after Hitler's invasion of Poland and his refusal to withdrawal after a British Declaration to Germany. At this point Hitler had already seized the Rhineland, Austria (the Anschluss) and Czechoslovakia. After Poland Hitler would go on to invade the remainder of northern and western Europe with the exception of Spain, where his fascist ally General Franco held sway, and Portugal, which remained neutral under Antonio de Oliveira Salazar, and hoped to keep the Nazis out of Portugal by exporting valuable war materials such as iron ore and tungsten to support Nazi Germany's war machine.

The worst of Hitler's devilish policy was his anti Semitic pogroms against not only the Jewish people of Germany also Jews in every country that Germany invaded. This pervasive evil culminated in what was described as "The Final Solution of the Jewish People" with the establishment in Germany and elsewhere of "Concentration Camps" where millions of innocent Jews were systematically murdered. Most were cremated after being typically gassed in horrific chambers where hundreds were gathered to be mercilessly killed. The full extent of these horrors would be exposed after the Allies' invasion of northern Europe and Germany and discovery of these camps.

The "Final Solution" was planned in meticulous detail at the January, 1942 Wannsee Conference. Nazi officials from a large number of German government departments were involved. Hitler gave his full approval. At the end of July, 1941 Hermann Goring authorized Reinhard Heydrich to plan the implementation of a "Complete Solution of the Jewish Question". This was the culmination of a decade of intensive state sanctioned vilification and persecution. The young Ben Ferencz grew up in 1920s and 1930s America in a caring and loving family that enjoyed the benefits of the world's premier democracy. Anti Semitism was unknown in his world in New York City and he enjoyed the benefits of an excellent education. Ben was intellectually gifted, as well as a hard working, and a dedicated student who was motivated to learn and do well. Ben Ferencz was an academic star. He excelled at Townsend Harris High School, where he was outstanding at French, and from there, in

1937, he won a free place to the City College of New York. In 1940 he graduated aged 20 with a Bachelor's degree in Social Sciences. He went to on from City College with a Federal Scholarship to Harvard Law School and graduated in early 1943. In the midst of his higher education the Japanese attacked the United States Pacific Fleet at Pearl Harbor on December 7, 1941. During the period 1942-1943 the United States waged war on two fronts, in the Pacific, and initially in north African and later northern Europe, with battles in Libya and Egypt following landings in Operation Torch in November, 1942. The United States Navy waged war together with the Royal Navy against the German Kriegsmarine in the North Atlantic.

While studying hard at Harvard the young Ben Ferencz was constantly aware of the war raging in Europe and in the Pacific. On graduation he enlisted in the United States Army. He landed in Europe on Omaha Beach after the D-Day landings on June 6, 1944, as part of the US Army's 115th Gun Battalion within the US Third Army under the command of General George Patton. Ben was part of the assault on Nazi Germany culminating in the German surrender. He became part of the Judge Advocate General's (JAG) organization, a natural event given his outstanding legal training

Alfred Jodl, Chief of Staff of the German Army, signed the unconditional surrender of the Third Reich in the early hours of Monday, May 7, 1945 at Supreme Headquarters, Allied Expeditionary Force (SHAEF) at Reims in northeastern France. The Germans surrendered unconditionally in the east on May 9, 1945. Victory in Europe Day (V-E Day) was officially proclaimed on May 8, 1945 with celebrations in Washington, London, Moscow, and Paris. Hitler had committed suicide in his command bunker in central Berlin on April 30, 1945 before the Soviet Army reached Berlin.

By the time of the surrender the young Ben Ferencz had seen the worst of war. His young and fine mind had ingrained memories of what it took for the Allies to liberate Europe and free people from the worst dictatorship imaginable. One experience was foremost in Ben's memory, something that no one could ever erase, whatever the help from counseling. He witnessed at first hand the horrors of the

Nazi concentration camps as the US Army marched into Germany. He saw the full evil of Nazi anti Semitism, something that he and no one could ever forget. He was there when the concentration camps were liberated. The emotional impact of this massive tragedy and man's inhumanity to man coupled with his newly acquired sense of justice would stay with Ben Ferencz for the rest of his life. All this not only scarred his emotions it created in him an everlasting sense of justice, that such evil had to be both punished and also prevented in the future. For the young lawyer no such evil could be allowed to be perpetrated in the future. For Ben there had to be a better way, a way to prevent the likes of Adolf Hitler and his massive entourage of evil doers from ever again perpetrating such evil, with the deaths of millions of innocent Jews, and the massive casualties suffered by the United States and the Allies in defeating Nazi Germany. At war's end in the spring of 1945 Ben Ferencz had no idea that very soon he would be called to serve again. Ferencz returned to the United States at the end of the war with thousands of other brave young Americans, bloodied in World War Two Europe. He was discharged as a Sergeant, United States Army. This was to change, very soon, totally unbeknown to Ben.

While Ben Ferencz recovered from his war experiences the United States and British leaderships were faced with the massive moral and legal issues surrounding the crimes committed by the Nazis against the Jewish people of Europe and Russia, together with other war crimes and crimes against humanity by the Germans as a whole. The latter included not just the Nazi personnel involved in the Jewish extermination operations and concentration camps, also those involved in the pre war German preparations and plans for war, as well as war operations 1939-1945. These crimes covered multiple locations and every element of the Nazi hierarchy and German armed forces, Army, Navy, and Air Force. The young Ferencz, fresh from an horrific war, was summoned to service again by the United States Army in 1946. He was ordered to become part of General Telford Taylor's War Crimes team, and given the civilian status as a prosecutor equivalent to a full colonel in the United States Army. At his age this was an extraordinary event. He shipped to Germany and soon found himself as a key prosecution member of the International Military Tribunal at Nuremberg, Germany, forever known as the Nuremberg War Crimes Trials.

In 1946 Ben Ferencz was given a hugely demanding responsibility. On March 11, 1946 Ben turned 26 years of age. His work in Nuremberg would not complete until 1948, requiring enormous intellectual, physical and emotional energy, resilience, and courage in the face of the most appalling evidence presented to the judges of the International Military Tribunal. All eyes at times were totally transfixed on Ferencz. What he experienced in Nuremberg fashioned the rest of his life and led in due course to major and lasting changes to the international legal and judicial system.

What was Ben Ferencz tasked with by General Telford Taylor and the International Military Tribunal? He became the Chief Prosecutor of what was called the "Einsatzgruppen" Tribunal. This composed the trial of the leading Nazis that led and orchestrated the murder and extermination of over 1 million Jews as the German Army, the Wehrmacht, invaded the Soviet Union. This special SS group was formed as a totally separate entity from the main German Army, most of whom had little or no knowledge of their organization, intent, and evil operations. In July, 1941, a month after the initial invasion of the Soviet Union, Hitler gave Heinrich Himmler the responsibility for overseeing all security measures in what would be the newly conquered areas of the Soviet Union. This included the authority to eliminate by whatever means he deemed necessary and perceived threats to German conquest and rule. Himmler sent reports to Hitler based on the "Einsatzgruppen"'s leadership's reports to him about the number of people executed as "Enemies of the Reich", including horrific details of the huge number of innocent Jewish civilians murdered by mass shootings. It is estimated that the Holocaust genocide saw the murder of approximately 6 million Jews across Europe. This horrendous evil policy of the Nazis equates to two thirds of the Jewish population in Europe and 90% of Polish Jews. The one million Jews and other ethnicities murdered by the Einsatzgruppen during the Nazi Soviet invasion may well be too low a number. The antecedents in Germany after 1933, when Hitler introduced a series of policies that subjected German Jews to discrimination and persecution set the stage for the world's worst genocide. In April, 1933 Jews were removed from the German Civil Service and government; on September 15, 1935 Jews were prohibited from marrying or having sexual relations with German people; on October 15, 1936 Jewish teachers were banned from teaching at schools; on April 9, 1937 Jewish children were not allowed to attend schools in Berlin; on October 5, 1938 German Jews must have the letter "J" stamped on their passport and Polish Jews were expelled from Germany. On November 7, 1938 a German politician was assassinated in Paris by a Polish-Jewish student named Herschel Grynszpan. Hitler and his Minister of Propaganda, Joseph Goebbels ordered a series of violent retaliations against Jews in Germany. These attacks became known as "Kristallnacht", ("Night of the Broken Glass", due to the amount of broken glass on the German streets the following day), now often referred to in modern Germany as "Reichspogromnacht", as the original term is regarded as too repugnant. Over 100 Jews lost their lives and 30,000 Jewish men were sent to prison camps.

This was the history that the young Ben Ferencz entered as the US Third Army liberated northern Europe and entered Nazi Germany. In addition to Jews the Einsatzgruppen also killed other racial groups such as gypsies that the dark powers within the Nazi party deemed unworthy to live. Such was the magnitude of the crimes committed by the leaders of this extermination group. The trial that Ben Ferencz led as Chief Prosecutor was described by the Associated Press as "The Biggest Murder Trial in History". He had already been involved in collecting evidence at concentration camps in Buchenwald, Ebensee, and Mauthausen. His prosecution team put together overwhelming and frightening evidence against all 22 officers of the SS (Schutzstaffel). All 22 SS officers were convicted and the leaders executed. Ernst Kaltenbrunner, the highest ranking surviving SS main department chief was also found guilty of crimes against humanity and hanged in 1946.

Ben's pivotal work at Nuremberg would have a lifelong effect on his life, career, and commitment to one critical domain, the preservation and pursuit of peace through international law, not war. He became, and still is after his passing, the model for the pursuit of peace through international law. Later in life he donated 200 archive boxes of documents, letters, and photos to the United States Holocaust Museum in Washington DC, with the firm hope that memories would never die of the atrocities committed and that the rule of international law prevailed. When he completed his work at Nuremberg in 1948, with all 22 defendants convicted, his life was now dedicated to the pursuit of peace through international law.

He stayed in Germany until 1956 working on restitution for Jewish people who were victims of Nazi war crimes. These years in Germany compounded his growing commitment to work towards establishing international institutions through the United Nations to protect the peoples of the world against war crimes and crimes against humanity. His work would culminate in 1998 with the Rome Statute and the establishment of the International Criminal Court (ICC) in The Hague, Netherlands.

After his Jewish restitution work Ben returned to the United States and settled in New Rochelle, New York, with his wife, Gertrude Fried, whom he had married in New York 1946 before he returned to Germany to work on the Nuremberg War Crimes trials. Ben and Gertrude were married for 73 years until she died in 2019. They had four children and Benjamin lived longer, passing away at an assisted living facility in Boynton Beach, Florida, on April 7, 2023, at the age of 103.

From 1956 until he succumbed to the effects of very old age, not long before his passing, Ben never gave up on his dedication to international law.

SIX

PRELUDE TO JUDGMENT AND THE NUREMBERG WAR CRIMES TRIALS

There were several dimensions and experiences that led to Ben Ferencz's critical role at the Nuremberg War Crimes Trials of the evil Einsatzgruppen (in English "Deployment Groups", also "Task Forces"). He not only had to deal with the procedures for the fair trial of the accused senior Nazi personnel responsible for the atrocities he also had to address his own inner sanctum, his own intellectual, emotional, and psychological conditions. These were complex and were imposed on a young gifted man with more than just a fine sense of duty, responsibility, and adherence to the rules of the International Military Tribunal at Nuremberg. Like Thousands of young Americans, British, and Canadian troops he had witnessed the horrors of war after landing in Normandy. He had seen the price paid on the battlefield for the liberation of Europe. The first Allied cemetery in Europe was dedicated just two days after the D-Day invasion of June 6th, 1944. Of the 4,414 Allied deaths on June 6th 1944 2,501 were Americans. With the injured the Allies suffered some 10,000 casualties just on D-Day itself. "Operation Overlord" was seared on Ben Ferencz's memory as he prepared his case at Nuremberg, together with other overwhelming experiences until the German surrender. Approximately 4,500,000 US and Allied troops were involved after D-Day in the advance into Germany. This number was composed of 91 Divisions, a number unprecedented, and perhaps unthinkable today in terms of modern warfare and the size and shape of the modern US Army and US Marine Corps. What Ben Ferencz experienced was one man as a small cog in a massive machine. He saw at close hand the losses and injuries of his fellow Americans. By the time the Germans surrendered the United States had lost 62,704 casualties, the British 17,930, and the Canadians 6,490. During the liberation campaign the French lost 18,306 and there were 715 casualties from other Allies round the world.

In 1945 and beyond there were no such words describing what today is the well known condition of PTSD, Post Traumatic Stress Disorder. Shell Shock during World War One had been slightly understood though its treatment very limited. There is little or no data describing what the brave and courageous Allied men who liberated Europe after D-Day truly suffered mentally as a result of their war experiences advancing after D-Day into Germany. Ben Ferencz was simply just one of thousands who witnessed the horrors of war, tempered perhaps by the welcoming people of non German Europe as they were liberated. These absolutely memorable and cheerful events across the villages, towns, and cities of northern Europe must have been such incredibly heart warming experiences after such hard fought battles as the Battle of the Bulge, and Operation Market Garden earlier in the Fall of 1944 to liberate and control the critical bridges across the Rhine. The Battle of Arnhem September 17-26 1944 has been immortalized as an example of courage and endurance and one of the greatest feats of arms of the Second World War. Today the bridge over the lower Rhine at Arnhem in the Netherlands is named after the commander of the British Parachute unit that held the bridge against overwhelming odds until forced to surrender. "John Frost Bridge" (after Major General John Dutton Frost, 1912-1993) today recalls one great feat of so many courageous US and Allied feats of arms. The Battle of the Bulge will remain one of the greatest feats of American arms.

All of these experiences seared into young Ben Ferencz's mind and emotions. How could they not? One such set of experiences perhaps above all others was to have a lasting effect on his life and commitment to justice. What happened occurred between landing on Omaha Beach in Normandy on June 10th 1944 and him appearing as the lead prosecutor in the Einsatzgruppen trials. Those American and Allied forces that liberated the Concentration Camps underwent the most appalling experiences. The sights they witnessed could never be forgotten and expunged from the memory bank of men who were both so young and brought up in every kind of American village, town, and city, from multitudes of backgrounds and economic and educational stations in life. The impact was the same: one of horror, disgust, and total pity for the millions of Jews murdered and incinerated.

When Ben Ferencz entered Flossenburg and Buchenwald Concentration camps in April-May, 1945 as a member of the US Third Army the sights were unbearable. He went on to Dachau and Mauthausen-Gusen concentration camps, where he began his investigations into Nazi war crimes. What he experienced in these few months fashioned his life. More was required from him than the natural reaction to punish the vast number of perpetrators of these atrocities. He had to step back and let his fine mind address all the complex legal issues that would be subsequently demanded of him, after his return to the United States at the end of the war and his subsequent return in April, 1946, after his appointment by Chief Prosecutor Colonel Telford Taylor to the prosecutorial staff of the International Military Tribunal at Nuremberg. The still very young Ben Ferencz now found that on May 2, 1945 President Harry S. Truman had appointed Associate Supreme Court Justice Robert H. Jackson as Chief Prosecutor for the United States at Nuremberg. President Truman gave Justice Jackson free rein to choose his own staff and to be a major player in the design and implementation of the unique trials about to take place in Nuremberg. When Colonel

Telford Taylor appointed the young Ben Ferencz he was given the civilian equivalent in rank, style and title of a Brigadier General, a one star officer, in the United States Army. In just a short time Ferencz went from being an enlisted soldier in the Third Army to a civilian Brigadier General equivalent at Nuremberg. When the case against the Einsatzgruppen opened, mid 1947 to April 1948 Ferencz had already done major research in Berlin into the accused. Justice Robert Jackson, Chief US Prosecutor at Nuremberg opened the prosecution case against the Einsatzgruppen accused, and Ferencz then proceeded to make the Opening Statement to the panel of judges and then lead the prosecution to its conclusion, with the conviction of all the accused.

The four Nuremberg judges were: Geoffrey Lawrence from the UK; Francis Biddle from the United States; Judge Henri Donnedieu de Vabres from France, and Ion Nikitchenko from the Soviet Union.

There were alternate judges to support the official four sitting judges, of which the British judge, later First Baron Norman Birkett, was the most distinguished and gave invaluable service to the four sitting judges. The US justice, Francis Biddle, conveyed great praise after the trials concluded for what he considered Birkett's invaluable support work at Nuremberg. The US alternate judge was John Parker; the French alternate judge was Robert Falco who spoke English and had served on France's highest court; the Soviet alternate judge was Alexander Volchkov who had a versatile background as a prosecutor, criminal judge, and a diplomat.

The young Ben Ferencz, war hardened, highly gifted intellectually, well trained at Harvard Law School, and a first hand witness to the horrendous war crimes committed by the Nazis, succeeded in every dimension required of a Nuremberg War Crimes prosecutor.

However, there was much more of significance to what he achieved at Nuremberg. He never ever forgot the impact of what he witnessed first hand. The psychological and emotional stress of war went beyond the fine judicial intellect of this outstanding young lawyer and soldier.

He became committed to a life's work dedicated to several key propositions. Above all he was a bastion for ensuring that peace, not war, prevailed. He dedicated the rest of his life to the pursuit of peace by nurturing and helping institute the principles of international law in the service of justice and freedom.

SEVEN

EVERLASTING RECOGNITION AND COMMITMENT TO THE PURSUIT OF PEACE

After his work on German Restitution (1948-1949) and Reparations from German industrialists (1950-1956) Ben Ferencz returned to New York City and the practice of law from 1956 to 1968. For Ben practicing regular law was not what both interested and motivated him. Within his fine intellect, experience base, and indeed inner soul was a commitment to finding better ways for the world to maintain peace while also ensuring that justice could be served at an international level for crimes that affected humanity as a whole. This became his guiding star, one that he never lost sight of throughout the rest of his life. In 1961 the talented American movie producer and director Stanley Kramer created the outstanding film "Judgment at Nuremberg". For the first time the vast majority of people who were not aware of either the Nuremberg War Crimes Trials and the background to the cases that were tried by the International Military Tribunal came into stark and enduring focus. The plot centered on the trial of Nazi judges that had subverted their judicial independence to the demands of Hitler and his Nazi Party. It was a fictionalized version of the trials of Nazi judges at Nuremberg in 1947. The judges were accused of unlawful sentencing of innocent Germans who were either not subservient to the Nazi Party or were, simply, Jewish. The movie showed how countless innocent accused were sentenced often to death based on zero evidence other than sheer political pressure and trumped up accusations of crimes against the Nazi state. The accused Nazi judges totally complied and were guilty of Crimes against Humanity. It is critical to stress that Stanley Kramer and his production team demonstrated to the unknowledgeable public worldwide just how despicable and evil was the regime that cost millions of lives. The movie was powerful in its message, with the added attraction of a star studded cast. The latter included Spencer Tracy, Burt Lancaster, Richard Widmark, Marlene Dietrich, Maximilian Schell, Judy Garland, Montgomery Clift, and William Shatner. This cast attracted a wide audience both in the United States and internationally. The message conveyed was clear and highly demonstrable in graphic terms. In 1961 when the movie was released Ben Ferencz was a relative unknown except for those who were either involved at Nuremberg, followed the cases and history as lawyers or academics, and those politicians who were aware of the sheer magnitude of the atrocities committed by the Nazis. Ben Ferencz was about to change this perspective, and dedicated the rest of his life's work to create the means to challenge those who committed War Crimes, Crimes against Humanity, and what later would be categorized as Human Trafficking and other illicit offences on an international, inter-state scale.

It is noteworthy to reflect that since "Judgment at Nuremberg's" 1961 release there has been no movie made that shows on the big screen the work of Ben Ferencz both at Nuremberg and all his subsequent contributions to the establishment of international law and institutions. His story is simply extraordinary and would make a wonderful movie in the current era. In one simple word such a movie would reflect Ben Ferencz's essence and huge contributions, "Inspirational". One of today's leading producers, together with a galaxy of contemporary stars could make an incredible movie, an international box office success in the making. In 1968, seven years after the movie's release, Ben Ferencz began his campaign of "Peace through Law". This would end perhaps in 1990 at one level, but would persist until July, 2002 for reasons that will become apparent. Ben Ferencz was a focused, dedicated, hard working lawyer with very clear objectives in mind. What were these as he started on his long journey? The seminal backdrop to Ben's dedicated work occurred on June 26, 1945 with the founding document of the United Nations, signed in San Francisco, at the conclusion of the United Nations Conference on International Organization. The United Nations Charter came into force on October 24, 1945. During World War Two President Franklin D. Roosevelt had a vision for the collective security of all nations in order to create an environment for lasting world peace and to deter and prevent both the causes of World War Two and the atrocities committed. When President Roosevelt died President Harry Truman continued his predecessor's dream and turned this into reality. The result was the United Nations Charter, with every member country contributing to the United Nations' budget, with mandatory contributions for administrative costs and peacekeeping operations. Other specific United Nations programs to this day receive voluntary contributions from member states. The essence of the United Nations was therefore to protect human rights, deliver humanitarian aid, uphold international law, as well as pursue current issues such as Climate Change and support sustainable development programs within the various nations.

Several key bodies were founded when the United Nations was established. These were the General Assembly, the Security Council, the Economic and Social Council, the Trusteeship Council, the United Nations Secretariat and, most important of all from Ben Ferencz's perspective, the International Court of Justice (ICJ). The United States has been the largest contributor to the United Nations, paying 22% of the regular budget and has been assessed as paying 27% of the peacekeeping budget. Much later, in 1993, the United States Congress placed a 25% maximum contribution or cap on US contributions to peacekeeping. There were 51 Founding Members of the United Nations in 1945. The UN Charter does provide for the expulsion of member nations. The Trusteeship Council suspended its operations on November 1, 1994, a month after the independence of Palau, the last remaining United Nations Trust Territory. Since 1948 the United Nations has helped end conflicts and promotes reconciliation through peacekeeping operations in dozens of countries around the world. For examples, just a few, in Cambodia, El Salvador, Guatemala, Mozambique, Namibia, and Tajikistan.

Ben Ferencz was in the midst of his intensive lead up to his work at Nuremberg when the United States led in the formation of the United Nations. He was totally preoccupied. What was to impact his later work came on December 10, 1948 with the "Universal Declaration of Human Rights", adopted by the new United Nations General Assembly, directly as a result of the experiences of World War Two and the war crimes trials of German and Japanese military and civilian leaders. The United Nations established sovereign equality of all the United Nations members was a key founding principle. After what in retrospect seems like his legal sojourn in New York City from 1956-1968 Ben Ferencz became inspired, very simple and very clearly to work with the United Nations and all the international legal allies that he could muster, to create a whole new environment and institutions beyond the International Court of Justice. This is where his visionary inspiration, dedication, unremitting zeal, and sheer persistence all combined with one key goal in mind. This goal was fashioned by his abiding World War Two experiences and a lead prosecutor at Nuremberg. What he wanted to achieve would take years of unremitting energy and working with legal allies at an international level. It is essential that underlying this unremitting commitment was one simple and crucial principle uppermost in his mind: "Peace Through Law". What Ferencz wanted would go beyond the United Nations International Court of Justice. What he wanted was an International Criminal Court, or ICC for short. This was his vision. How did he do this between 1968, and from 1990 onwards, creating at the United Nations the ideal that an ICC was vital for world peace. He spent all these years assiduously working to this end, never giving up, never being subject to negative pressures and opposing legal arguments, always staying focused on that one single objective. In Churchillian phrase, "He never gave up, and he never surrendered". Step by step, stage by stage, he systematically worked at the United Nations to rally support, year after year.

On May 25, 1993 he witnessed his major break through in the United Nations international legal system with the creation of the International Criminal Tribunal for the former Yugoslavia. This was the first major step to his ultimate triumph. In 1995 the United Nations created the Rome Convention for establishing an International Criminal Court (ICC). One of Ben Ferencz's proudest moments and one of his finest achievements, indeed perhaps in Churchillian phrase, "His Finest Hour" was his magnificent address to the Rome Convention. He did not end there. He wanted to ensure the ultimate success. On April 11, 2002, after his further prodigious work, the United Nations ratified the work of the Rome Convention and then came the finale, on July 1, 2002, the United Nations Treaty creating the International Criminal Court went into full effect. Benjamin Ferencz's decades of hard work was fulfilled. The United Nations International Criminal Court was established in The Hague, Netherlands, with 8 judges, a full legal staff, and other critical administrative and investigatory staff. The latter would be linked to the international investigative arms and organizations of the member states. The young man that had been a lead prosecutor at the Nuremberg War Crimes Trials had now fulfilled what may be considered his life's work. This was a massive achievement. Ben Ferencz never gave up after what would seem like the ultimate triumph. He would continue after the founding of the ICC to dedicate himself to the preservation of Human Rights at all levels, including the Rights of Women, freedom of speech and religion, and the rights to have sexual choice and gender. When he passed away in 2023 Benjamin Ferencz leaves an incredible legacy that must endure. His legal and personal spirit abides today in the halls of not just the International Criminal Court also in all the myriad legal institutions, legal chambers, courts and law schools of the free world. His work will abide for all time.

Ferencz in the Harvard Law Library in 1942.

Ferencz as a U.S. army corporal, 1943.

Ferencz at the podium for the prosecution's opening statement in the Einsatz-gruppen Tribunal (USHMM Photo #09917).

The defendants sit in the dock at the Einsatzgruppen Trial (USHMM Photograph #16813).

Ferencz addressing the Rome Convention for the establishment of an International Criminal Court in 1998.

In The Hague, Benjamin Ferencz (left) and Antonio Cassese (right) are honored with the prestigious Erasmus Peace prize by Prince Willem-Alexander of The Netherlands.

EIGHT

A LASTING LEGACY FOR OUR TIMES IN AN AGE OF GREAT STRESS AND INTERNATIONAL DISORDER AND CRISIS

The work of Benjamin Ferencz is as important today as it was during the years of his legal triumphs. Now, in 2023, the year of his passing, the world is experiencing great stress, international disorder, and crisis. How would he look at world affairs today and what should we do in response to the international challenges that we face? Let us first look at the greatest challenges that we face today and then how should we build on Ben Ferencz's great work and consider the means to implementation. One critical observation is that Extremism is rampant throughout the modern World. Women in Iran are being vilified, imprisoned, tortured, and murdered for holding forth fundamental rights. Syria harbors a despotic regime that undermines core human values and rights, and North Korea is home to not just an extremist regime also one that is employing nuclear weapons as an instrument of extreme nationalism and ideological paranoia. China is a single party regime with total surveillance and controls over its population with zero means for the growth of change and democratic institutions. Russia commenced an illegal and brutal war against Ukraine in February, 2022 against all the established conventions of the United Nations and the International Court of Justice. Russia' s leader, Vladimir Putin, and his cohorts, have committed war crimes against the Ukrainian people in violations of the Geneva Conventions, the Rules of War, and the International Criminal Code for crimes against Humanity and War Crimes. The world has watched brutal extremism unfold daily throughout 2022 and 2023 via often real time television and radio broadcasts. Innocent men, women and children have been brutally murdered. This is Extremism of the worst kind. These events bring back stark memories and thoughts about Nazi atrocities and the Nuremberg War Crimes Trials. For many it is almost unimaginable that this is happening, here in our world, in 2023. How could this be and what do we need to do to put our world back in good order?

On October 7th 2023 Hamas brutally attacked innocent Israeli citizens, murdering 1,200 people. The military response from Israel has left well over 20,000 dead in Gaza, including a large number of totally innocent men, women, and children, with the destruction of homes, schools, and hospitals. The Israeli-Hamas conflict will be addressed in detail later. Ben Ferencz would have made significant commentary on this conflict as well as Russia's attack on Ukraine. He would have found the reactions and actions of Russia, Hamas, and Israel as intolerable. Extremism can take lesser forms, and these may have over the course of time the potential for negative change in a democratic society. January 6, 2021 in Washington DC at the heart of American democracy showed in graphic terms what may happen. Prevention is always better than cure. It is better to know what and when extremist threats develop, their nature, location, and intent, than to wait until the worst case occurs. There is a divide between Extremism and terrorism. However if Extremism develops into regimes that have the potential for violent outcomes to facilitate change then this automatically verges on, and may metamorphose into terrorism.

In January, 2023, two years after the Capitol insurrection of January 6, 2021, the United States was still struggling to deal with the fallout from that momentous day in US history. On Friday, January 6, 2023 President Joseph Biden honored those who had bravely defended the United States Capitol from the violent attacking insurgents.

The loved ones of those who made the supreme sacrifice with their lives were given special honors. The media later observed the absence of opposition party members at the ceremony, a totally non partisan event, other than the presence of one member from the Republican Party. The divisiveness was reinforced later that day by the prolonged process that led to the election of the new Speaker of the US House of Representatives, a process that night fraught with acrimony and negotiation with individual members of Congress with records that showed that they had supported the false claims about the 2020 Presidential election results and in certain cases had attended the insurgency.

The 118th US Congress was therefore officially convened on that day. The progress of this Congress in the House of Representatives until dissolution in January, 2025 will bear very special observation. Kevin McCarthy, Republican from California, was elected Speaker after a tortuous series of votes and negotiations characterized by considerable rancor exacerbated by several individual extremists on the far right of the Republican party. He would be later replaced in a highly contentious series of alarming events. By contrast Hakeem Jeffries from New York became the first Black leader of the Democratic Party in the House of Representatives, making a resounding speech in the early hours of Saturday, January 7, 2023 for national unity in order to serve the American people. The moderation of the Democratic party was observed by the media and the world via C-Span in stark contrast to the vituperative negotiations made within the Republican party with Extremists to ensure the election of Speaker McCarthy. By contrast on the Senate side Democrat Patty Murray became the President Pro tempore. It remains to be seen how between 2023 and 2025 the Rules Committee of the US House of Representatives, led by a new Speaker in late 2023 of the House, will interact over the major issue of investigations. Of concern within the context of extremism are attacks by investigation on both the Federal Bureau of Investigation (FBI) and the US Department of Justice (DOJ) at the behest of a minority of extremists within the Republican party. Of concern is the proliferation of such actions to more moderate members who may see future re-election benefits in congressional districts where voters may approve of and want their representative to support such activities. The FBI and the DOJ are two cornerstones that uphold not just federal law and order they also are two critical guardians of the intrinsic democratic institutions of the United States. Nazi Germany in the 1930s showed how good people made catastrophic decisions to support measures that in due course led to the undermining of the well established law enforcement institutions of the Weimar Republic. The result was the later creation of three demonic organizations, the SS (Schutzstaffel), the SD (Sicherheitsdienst), and the notorious Gestapo (Geheime Staatspolizei). These subverted traditional law and order organizations and undermined the judicial system and its independence from political influence. This is extreme and hopefully nothing even approaching it may ever occur in the United States. Ben Ferencz was only too aware of how this process can work and how democracy can be subverted and within a relatively short time become a dictatorial despotism. The champion of international law would tell us today that things may happen in ways that seem outlandish and impossible. He would say "Tell that to the German people in 1933, and then ask them what they faced 1933-1939". It seems outlandish to even contemplate let alone its possibility. What is important to observe is the mechanism of extremism, the various stages, and the ways and means by which traditional well established institutions may be undermined, even if they never reach the extreme variants described above. It is the process away from well established democratic procedures to more extreme measures that need to be understood and guarded against. Traditionally solid and dependable institutions and the multifarious sections of society that traditionally are perfectly stable, decent, honest, law abiding, with strong positive values, can be influenced as Ben Ferencz would emphasize, and then controlled by extremist forces. Once control is obtained the slippery slope to despotism and totalitarianism, with the very worst heinous anti Semitic and racist policies ensuing. All this may seem fanciful, but it happened in Europe, and can happen again.

The US government led by the Biden administration has made strides in combating domestic terrorism. However, this appears to have been done without any consensus in sight regarding domestic terrorism legislation, and federal agencies remain without crucial tools and resources needed to comprehensively address future threats from extremist movements, groups, and organizations. This may reflect both political diversity and also institutional lethargy and inability to gain a consensus.

Since the attack on the Capitol, militia violent extremists present on January 6th, including the Oath Keepers and the Three Percenters, have mostly assumed a lower profile, opting to go dormant to avoid further scrutiny. The United States has become a net exporter of anti-government and anti-authority extremism, and January 6th has become a rallying cry and symbol for accelerationists and violent extremists abroad.

Although the Capitol insurrection of January 6, 2021, did not fuel a wave of violence, it has left an indelible scar on political processes and discourse in the United States, which is still struggling to deal with the fallout from that day. The absence of widespread violence is partly due to the proactive measures taken by law enforcement and criminal justice authorities to investigate, arrest, and prosecute those individuals who committed crimes related to the attempted overthrow of the U.S. government. As of January 2023, more than 950 individuals linked to the Capitol attack had been arrested and charged with crimes, according to a recent press release from the Department of Justice. Yet, despite the best efforts of the January 6th Committee, which outlined in painstaking detail the role played by former U.S. President Donald Trump and his allies in provoking the insurrection, none has been held accountable for their actions. Accordingly, there is little incentive to cease spewing divisive rhetoric, even as the Department of Homeland Security has repeatedly warned of a heightened threat environment The rhetoric has being far from harmless; rather, it has visibly corroded the electoral process by introducing doubts about the validity of the system. In an era of disproportionate noise-to-signal ratios, exacerbated by social media and encrypted chat rooms, there is a growing recognition that the most nefarious threat could emanate from the so-called "dogs that don't bark." In other words, there are widespread fears within the intelligence and law enforcement communities of an Oklahoma City-style domestic terrorism attack targeting U.S. government employees and facilities. The Biden administration has made genuine and laudable strides in combating domestic terrorism, formulating a strategy that encompasses four pillars: understanding and sharing domestic terrorism-related information; preventing recruitment and mobilization to violence; disrupting and deterring domestic activity before it can metastasize; and attempting to deal with some of the core drivers, including polarization, disinformation, and the spread of violent conspiracy theories. However, there is no consensus in sight regarding domestic terrorism legislation that would give the Federal Bureau of Investigation (FBI) and other government agencies important tools and resources needed to properly counter the threat in its various manifestations. Lawmakers cannot even agree on who was to blame for the insurrection, with far-right members of Congress incredulously asserting that January 6th was a "false flag" operation orchestrated by "Antifa" and "radical Leftists," despite all the evidence brought forth since. Rampant disinformation and conspiracy-mongering have supplanted civil discourse and data-driven analysis. Added to this, and particularly as the November, 2024 US elections come into sight, is the threat of Artificial Intelligence (AI) supported disinformation, playing false data and images for political purposes. Few terrorism analysts remain sanguine that the underlying threat has receded. The individual who placed pipe bombs outside of both the Republican and Democratic party headquarters, respectively, has still not been identified. Furthermore, the QAnon conspiracy movement that inspired numerous individuals to attack the Capitol has evolved and continues to motivate real-world acts of violence and sow doubts about the credibility of the electoral system in the U.S. On the other hand, militia violent extremists who were present in large numbers on January 6th, including the Oath Keepers and the Three Percenters, have assumed a far lower public profile, preferring instead to drop off the radar in an effort to avoid further scrutiny or penalty. Many have received long sentences in US Federal courts. Ben Ferencz would approve of these judicial actions, exemplifying the rule of law in challenging times. The broader far-right ecosystem, from which many of the most radicalized insurrectionists emerged, continues to produce domestic terrorists that threaten the safety and security of American citizens, especially minority communities. In May 2022, a far-right terrorist killed ten people in a Buffalo grocery store, deliberately selected because it was located in a predominantly African American neighborhood. In addition to racially and ethnically motivated violent extremists (REMVE), anti-government and anti-authority violent extremists remain a top-tier threat to U.S. government entities, law enforcement personnel, and members of the U.S. military. Many terrorism analysts abroad consider that the United States has become a net exporter of anti-government and anti-authority extremism, inspiring and motivating sympathizers in many countries around the world. The events and narratives of January 6th have become a rallying cry and symbol for accelerationists and violent extremists abroad. From Latin America to Europe, citizens have sought common cause with U.S.-based extremists, latching on to a litany of far-right grievances in an effort to promote anti-government sentiment in their home countries. Reflecting the transnational nature of the threat, UN Secretary-General António Guterres recently published his first report on the rising international threat of far-right terrorism, highlighting the threat perceived by many states and the potential to address them through multilateral cooperation. Echoing TSC research and analysis, Avril Haines, the U.S. Director of National Intelligence (DNI), said that although the U.S. intelligence community has not yet identified an "operational nexus" between domestic violent extremism in the U.S. and foreign actors abroad, there is "a social media kind of ideological nexus." There are concerns that this dynamic could change, especially if malign state actors such as Russia – particularly after the boasts of Yevgeny Prigozhin, now the late the head of the private military company, the Wagner Group, of interfering in US elections - actively promote linkages and connections between far-right extremists globally. He died in a mysterious plane crash in Russia that many attribute to Vladimir Putin.

- The supporters of Brazil's former President, Jair Bolsonaro, stormed government buildings and institutions in ways similar to the U.S. Capitol insurrection of January 6, 2021. Prior to the Brazilian crisis various social media channels had been flooded with violent rhetoric and calls to wreak havoc throughout the country, as far-right extremists threatened attacks against infrastructure. The similarities to January 6th in the United States were stark. Bolsonaro's supporters characterized themselves as "patriots" in ways very similar to U.S. media exchanges personalities and those who had challenged the US election results.

The following statement by a distinguished former member of the Central Intelligence Agency (CIA) bears review. It is reproduced here as written:

- "During my 26-year career at the Central Intelligence Agency, my colleagues and I believed strongly in congressional oversight. As a case officer and then manager across three areas of responsibility (the Middle East, counterterrorism, and Europe), I spent considerable time with members of Congress and their staff. We always ensured that Congress was fully briefed on our traditional collection operations as well as covert action programs, and I considered Congress not as enemy territory but rather as national security colleagues. Congressional oversight is a key component of how the CIA operates. Most importantly, oversight can provide a solid mechanism for making the agency better, as Congress can be an effective change agent.

- With that in mind, I'm concerned about House Speaker Kevin McCarthy's possible creation of a MAGA-inspired subcommittee of the Judiciary Committee. A subcommittee that will go after the FBI, the Department of Justice, and the intelligence community. The name of this entity appears to be out of a bad spy novel - the committee on the "Weaponization of the federal government." It bears memory of actions by another former member of Congress named McCarthy.

- These developments are head-spinning if one knows the history between U.S. political parties and the national security establishment. Conservatives used to be the defenders of the FBI and CIA. The Left was the skeptic. What a flip. But what really matters is that a partisan circus around this Church-like committee will harm U.S. national security. Chinese intelligence is eating our lunch every day in the U.S. FBI Director Chris Wray has stated that the FBI opens an investigation on Chinese intelligence operations every 12 hours. So the GOP's answer is to attack and defund the FBI? This is being tough on China, as the new GOP House majority insists it is? Give me a break.

- Top line: a highly distracted FBI and intelligence community cannot do their jobs, which are to protect the people against threats from Russia, China, Iran, and terrorism. The manpower of our national security institutions is not limitless. Spurious fishing expeditions — which is not real oversight focused on specific concerns — will no doubt distract. We need FBI agents on the street, running surveillance operations against Chinese intelligence and recruiting their officers. We need the FBI and CIA penetrating terrorist groups. We need the NSA figuring out how to get inside encrypted Russian communication networks.

- I also worry about what message this sends to those who are interested in national security careers. Look at the terrible issues of hiring and retention that police departments face after the nonsense of the "defund the police" movement. We don't need this for those prospective FBI agents or CIA officers. Do we really want these talented young individuals to look at a Congressional charade and think, why bother?

- Historians will note that the political Right has despised the Church Committee as having de-fanged the intelligence community and ultimately led to significant intelligence failures. In fact, howling that the CIA had lost its mojo prior to Sept. 11, 2001, conservatives pointed directly to the Church Committee.

- What we need to see is moral courage by those in the Republican Party who understand that necessary oversight and partisan theatrics are not the same thing. They must step up now before it all goes totally off the rails. That means folks such as Brian Fitzpatrick, a former FBI agent. Same with Don Bacon, a former U.S. Air Force brigadier general. The head of the new China Select Committee, Mike Gallagher. Mike Waltz, a former Green Beret. Mike McCaul, chairman of the Foreign Affairs Committee. Will these voices speak up collectively as the 118th Congress takes shape? Will they vote against this rules legislation this week, or force the speaker to make changes?

- Moral courage is required to make sure this charade doesn't get dangerous. I'm all for congressional oversight. The existing intelligence oversight committees do that effectively. But a new Church Committee is not the answer."

- The author of the above was Marc Polymeropoulos, a non-resident senior fellow at the Atlantic Council. A former CIA senior operations officer, he retired in 2019 after a 26-year career serving in the Near East and South Asia. His book Clarity in Crisis: Leadership Lessons from the CIA was published in June 2021 by Harper Collins.

Whatever readers' political persuasions and voting loyalties, and leaving aside US party political issues the author raised key issues. These issues should be borne in mind as Ben Ferencz's life and work are set against these critical issues.

On a more lighthearted note the wonderfully sardonic and amusing comments below reflect the critical roles that the United States has played in preserving the intrinsic democratic values of the Free World.

Once upon a time when politicians did not tend to apologize for the United States' prior actions, herewith a refresher on how some former US patriots handled negative comments about the great country that is the United States:

- JFK'S Secretary of State, Dean Rusk, was in France in the early 60's when DeGaulle decided to pull out of NATO. DeGaulle said he wanted all US military out of France as soon as possible. Rusk responded: "Does that include those who are buried here?" DeGaulle did not respond. You could have heard a pin drop.

When in England, at a fairly large conference, Colin Powell was asked by the Archbishop of Canterbury if US plans for Iraq were just an example of "Empire Building' by President George Bush. He answered by saying, "Over the years, the United States has sent many of its fine young men and women into great peril to fight for freedom beyond our borders. The only amount of land we have ever asked for in return is enough to bury those that did not return." You could have heard a pin drop. There was a conference in France where a number of international engineers were taking part, including French and American. During a break, one of the

French engineers came back into the room saying, "Have you heard the latest dumb stunt Bush has done? He has sent an aircraft carrier to Indonesia to help the tsunami victims. What does he intend to do, bomb them?" A Boeing engineer stood up and replied quietly: "Our carriers have three hospitals on board that can treat several hundred people; they are nuclear powered and can supply emergency electrical power to shore facilities; they have three cafeterias with the capacity to feed 3,000 people three meals a day, they can produce several thousand gallons of fresh water from sea water each day, and they carry half a dozen helicopters for use in transporting victims and injured to and from their flight deck. We have eleven such ships; how many does France have?" You could have heard a pin drop.

A U.S. Navy Admiral was attending a naval conference that included Admirals from the US., English, Canadian, Australian and French Navies. At a cocktail reception, he found himself standing with a large group of officers that included personnel from most of those countries. Everyone was chatting away in English as they sipped their drinks, but a French admiral suddenly complained that, whereas Europeans learn many languages, Americans learn only English. He then asked, "Why is it that we always have to speak English in these conferences rather than speaking French?" Without hesitating, the American Admiral replied, "Maybe it's because the Brit's, Canadians, Aussie's and Americans arranged it so you wouldn't have to speak German." You could have heard a pin drop.

Finally, Robert Whiting, an elderly gentleman of 83, arrived in Paris by plane. At French Customs, he took a few minutes to locate his passport in his carry on. "You have been to France before, monsieur?" the customs officer asked sarcastically. Mr. Whiting admitted that he had been to France previously. "Then you should know enough to have your passport ready." The American said, "The last time I was here, I didn't have to show it." "Impossible.

Americans always have to show their passports on arrival in France !" The American senior gave the Frenchman a long hard look. Then, he quietly explained, "Well, when I came ashore at Omaha Beach on D-Day in 1944 to help liberate this country, I couldn't find a single Frenchman to show a passport to." You could have heard a pin drop. Ben Ferencz would wish that the great democratic traditions of the United States be preserved.

What issues would he wished addressed as priorities?

This is the moment in time when his life's work should come into focus.

As one of the creator's of the International Criminal Court (ICC) and the role of international justice in keeping peace in the world Ben Ferencz. First and foremost he believed that the ICC sets a standard, backed by a strong institutional philosophy and organization, both in The Hague where the court sits, and at the United Nations in New York. He would want exemplary standards set and every political means used to ensure that the ICC is allowed to perform its primary role as the guardian of international law to prosecute those who commit war crimes, crimes against humanity and associated acts such as human trafficking and terrorist acts. The precedent of Nuremberg supported by solid case law since the establishment of the United Nations' International legal system is the bedrock of what Ben Ferencz saw as the way to preserve peace and punish violators.

The warrant issued by the ICC for the arrest of Vladimir Putin exemplifies the need for even a head of state to be called to account in spite of legal arguments about personal immunity for a Head of State. Would the Nuremberg War Crimes Trials have given Hitler such head of state immunity if he had lived to be put on trial. Highly unlikely. Hitler committed suicide in his Berlin bunker to avoid such a trial.

An article in the November, 2023 edition of "Counsel" magazine, the official journal of the Barristers of England and Wales, by James

Onalaja, examined in detail the issues associated with heads of state being prosecuted by the ICC. He is an international law and human rights Barrister, appointed to the Lists of Counsel at the International Criminal Court and the Kosovo Specialist Chambers in The Hague and he chaired the International Criminal Court Bar Association Amicus Committee 2022-2023. He makes a profound case with which Ben Ferencz would absolutely agree. Regarding Putin he writes, "The instigation of criminal cases against Russian high officials such as Putin accompanied by arrest warrants by either of the proposed tribunals, consistent with international law, will send a clear message to others in positions of power, authority and influence across Russia, as well as the Russian population, the international community's determined resolve to ensure that impunity has no place regarding the atrocities in Ukraine and further, that there is no future for Russia among the community of nations with Putin at the helm. Such initiation of criminal cases before international tribunals was the beginning of the end for Milosevic, Milutinovic, and Taylor, and is highly likely to be the same for Putin. The mutiny by the Wagner mercenaries and Putin's apparent impotence is arguably a demonstration of this fact".

These are the words and assessments of a fine international lawyer practicing in The Hague. Putin will clearly have to be deposed, arrested, and with the agreement of the Russian government transported to The Hague to stand trial for his crimes. This may seem unrealistic in late 2023. However, before D-Day and at the height of Nazi oppression in Europe it would certainly have seemed a far away ideal that the Nazi leadership would eventually be put on trial in Nuremberg. All things are possible.

This is a fitting end to this tribute to the life and work of Benjamin Ferencz. He achieved so much in his 103 years. His guiding star remained constant throughout his life, dedicated to the proposition that international law can be a crucial bedrock in pursuing and preserving peace. We and the world owe him a lasting debt, inspired by his fortitude, resilience, intellectual eminence, and never giving up and yielding when things looked impossible.

He is a monument to preserving peace by judicial means in a well ordered and supported international legal system.

We all owe him so much.

Thank you Benjamin Ferencz for your life and work.

NINE

ART AS AN INSTRUMENT OF PEACE

Art over the centuries has been a critical transformational factor reflecting societies' history, culture, and development, long before the printing press was invented and people could read. Art over the past centuries from Greek and Roman times, through the Middle Ages, into the Renaissance, and through to today tells us about the essence of a country's development and their people. The great artists whose works today grace the galleries of the world and private collections tell us about the key factors underpinning each and every society.

Art in all its many diversities is a complex subject to reduce to a single description of how it has impacted and reflects the maintenance of peace. Art comes in so many different forms, from drawings, paintings, and buildings that visually has expressed to people over the centuries the thoughts and feelings of the artists. Art is a binding medium, and before modern telecommunications and transport systems, back in the age of sail and when the horse was the fasted means of land transportation, uniting people by expressing not just the individual artist's feelings, also a deep reflection of the times. In the modern era Picasso has had a huge influence on thought and feelings about peace and war. He made the "Dove" for example, the symbol of peace. Within Picasso's art are symbols of expression of peace, love, devotion to higher values, and the purity of the human spirit and soul beyond human earthly existence. Many other artists, such as Mohan Kumar have portrayed the bird on canvas representing peace, with a clear objective to sooth and heal the troubled thoughts and issues of individuals as well as society as a whole. Many artists over the centuries strove to provide renewal for each individual looking at their art. Much Indian art for example seeks to quieten the mind, capture a divine spirit and restore tranquility and peace.

Art then is a transformational and unifying force for peace and good. The idea of brotherhood is a strong unifying force in much global art. The creation of "Peace" is central. A world without discrimination has been a central theme in much global art.

Violence and hatred have been challenged by artists who are peace advocates. In much Asian art for example the innocence of the child and the scent of the lotus fills the canvases of many artists, In Europe art has represented often the end of war and hostilities between nations, a gift symbolizing a new beginning after conflict, such as the peace negotiations between Spain and England at the time of the reign of Charles the First in England. Art showed the positive effects of peace, with the olive branch joining with the dove as a powerful symbol of peace. Artists across the centuries have sought to show through their works the symbols of reconciliation, healing between enemies, and peaceful coexistence between nations and individuals who fought against each other. After World War Two the British Royal Air Force legendary Battle of Britain fighter pilot, the legless hero, Douglas Bader, reunited in peace with his erstwhile key enemy in the German Luftwaffe, symbolic of what was also commonplace in ancient Greek and Roman cultures. The olive branch was literally held out as a huge gesture of peace and goodwill. It was meant to indicate that the art of peace begins with each individual.

At another totally different level, without confusing words and meaning, there is also the "Art of War". In other words, in the context of "Peace", war should be avoided by diplomacy and, if unavoidable, such as the Nazi invasion and occupation of northern Europe, it should be conducted to minimizing damage and the loss of unnecessary life. This is where the great work of Benjamin Ferencz intersects with art, in establishing codes of conduct for war and ensuring that through international legal mechanisms, such as the Geneva Conventions and the Rules of War, that the innocent are protected. Ben Ferencz would agree with Albert Einstein that "Peace cannot be kept by force; it can only be achieved by understanding". Art exposes the cruelty of war, and therefore the alternative value of peaceful coexistence. On April 26, 1937 the Basque town of Guernica was firebombed by German led Fascist Forces. The attack killed hundreds of defenseless citizen. Pablo Picasso was ignited by this appalling attack, reminiscent of recent attacks on the civilians of Gaza, perhaps as many as 12,000 innocent non combatant men, women, and children, killed while the real enemy hid from the attacks. Picasso's 25 feet long painting "Guernica" reveals the savagery of the attack, a mesmerizing symbol of evil, with an underlying theme that "Peace" must prevail.

In similar vein the Polish born American artist Arthur Szyk satirized and belittled tyrants, such as Adolph Hitler, the Italian dictator Benito Mussolini, and the Japanese Emperor, Hirohito. They were presented as despotic bullies. His art and that of countless other artists over the centuries expose not just the cruelty of war, also the intense need to keep and preserve peace. Art then is a hugely formative means for the preservation of peace, instilling in those who stand and gaze at art in its many forms the need for peace and the avoidance of war. September 21st every year is the United Nations declared International Day of Peace, dedicating the day to the ideals of peace. Many contemporary artists, such as the African American Kaaria Mucherera symbolizes in his oil and acrylic art the desire for peace, with the bird of peace unifying the diverse religions of the world. Like Picasso in his day these contemporary artist continue the great tradition of Picasso in seeking to secure peace in the world. Photography is part of the art of peace and war. Perhaps one of the best illustrations of this are the photographs taken during the Great War of 1914-1918, particularly the photos of the Christmas Day Truce of 1914, with carol singing in the trenches and both sides venturing into "No Man's Land" to mingle with their enemies and exchange gifts. Although a single event such photographs along with thousands of other war related photos symbolize both the horrors of war and the hopes and ideals for peace. During the 1930s and throughout World War Two the Nazis in Germany stole and expropriated a massive amount of Jewish art. The series "Woman in Gold", on Netflix, is a true story about the Viennese art of Gustav Klimt, starring Helen Mirren and Ryan Reynolds. The movie was released in 2015. Mirren plays the role of Maria Altmann, an elderly Jewish refugee living in Cheviot Hills, Los Angeles. The series shows how with her young and capable lawyer, Randy Schoenberg, they fought the government of Austria for almost a decade to reclaim Gustav Klimt's iconic painting of her aunt, Adele Bloch-Bauer, "Woman in Gold". The painting had been stolen by the Nazis in Vienna just prior to World War Two, fifty years earlier, and they seek to reclaim ownership of the extremely valuable painting. Altman took her legal battle all the way to the United States Supreme Court, which rules on the case "Republic of Austria V. Altmann" (2004). Five paintings were covered, including three landscapes. The decisions by the US Supreme Court and Austrian arbitrators covered all five paintings. In June, 2006 Altman sold "Portrait of Adele Bloch-Bauer" to Ronald Lauder's Neue Galerie in New York for $135 million, setting a new mark for such works of art. Within five months Altman sold a companion painting at auction to Oprah Winfrey for almost $88 million, then the third highest priced painting., This story reflects a key theme that is strongly associated with the work and ideals of Benjamin Ferencz and his goal to restore "Peace" not just through international legal institutions and practices, also a process of "Restitution". Art "Provenance" of the recorded history of an artwork from its origin through many owners to the present is a major challenge in terms of locating the original owner or owners, such as those many German Jewish families and individuals who had their, in some cases priceless, art stolen from them. Many such owners either died in concentration camps or fled abroad without their personal possessions to escape the pogroms. Collectors and art dealers have played over the decades since World War Two a major role in this process.

The earlier history of collections such as the Elgin Marbles reveal how such art has become contentious not just at the family and personal level also at the international level between nations over the critical issue of original ownership. The British and Greek governments disagree on who owns the Elgin Marbles, housed in London at the British Museum. The Parthenon Marbles have been visited by a massive unknown number of visitors over the centuries. Since Greece gained independence from the Ottoman Empire in 1832 the Greek government has wanted them returned. Nazi thefts in the 1930s and during World War Two are in a wholly different category. Provenance research demands intensive investigation into a multiple sources and locations, such as wills, archives, and receipts from art transactions, auction sales, and art dealers' records. Tracking down original ownership is a hugely demanding task. The investigator has to look at exhibitions, galleries, public and private, auction catalogues, and any information available about the original artist and customer cum patron. Proof therefore of provenance is extremely difficult, time consuming, and costly. Nazi art looters were very simply thieves of the most evil kind. Here is one example of a Nazi theft, provenance, and restitution. The sculpture of St. John the Baptist was taken from Jakob and Rosa Oppenheimer in 1933 by the Nazis, sold at auction in 1937, and later ended up in the Landesmuseum in Wurttemberg. In 2011 the Oppenheimer heirs succeeded in having the sculpture restituted, and in 2012 the Getty bought the sculpture at auction. The Getty Research Institute has helped in researching and digitizing stolen art by the Nazis. The latter had several nefarious goals in seizing so much art from Jewish owners, one of which was to control the culture heritage of Europe. Nazi crimes, provenance, and restitution intertwine in the life and work of Ben Ferencz. He worked assiduously on restitution issues in post World War Two Germany. Art that was illegally and forcibly purloined many years ago is still today a live issue. Ben Ferencz's work in being a major leading creator of the international legal system has set a benchmark in how such issues may be resolved. In his pursuit of peace Ben ensured that we have institutions in place that today are critical in ensuring that wrongdoing in the Russia-Ukraine and Israel-Hamas crisis does not go unpunished.

TEN

PUTTING WRONG RIGHT IN THE INTERNATIONAL ART WORLD

It will not be easy to put all the multitude of art thefts right so many decades after either their thefts or relatively peaceful and non criminal acts centuries ago by various nations. The leading question for the nations of the world is how may this be done?

The late 2023 controversy between the British and Greek governments over British retention of the Elgin Marbles in the British Museum in London shows how powerful this matter is. Thomas Bruce, the 7th Earl of Elgin, between 1801 and 1812 took this wonderful collection of ancient Greek sculptures from the Parthenon and other structures from the Acropolis in Athens and had them shipped to London. The majority of the sculptures were created in the 5th century BC under the direction of the sculptor and architect Phidias. The accuracy and veracity of Lord Elgin's claim that they were removed with the permission of the ruling Ottoman (Turkish) regime in Athens at the time has been disputed. Many leading British figures have questioned the removal of the Elgin Marbles, including Lord Byron, who described Elgin's actions as nothing short of vandalism or looting of another country's art treasures. In 1816 a British parliamentary inquiry concluded that

Elgin had acquired the marbles legally. Elgin sold them to the British government and a trusteeship was created with the British Museum. In 1983 the Greek government asked the British government for their return to Greece. The Greek government enlisted the help of UNESCO, and the UK government and British Museum declined UNESCO's offer of mediation. In 2021 UNESCO requested further inter governmental discussions. The British appear to have avoided the meeting. In 2023 the UK Prime Minister avoided a meeting with the Greek Prime Minister on this issue. Prime Minister Rishi Sunak told members of the UK House of Commons on November 29, 2023 that he had cancelled a planned meeting with Kyriakos Mitsotakis in London the day before because the Greek prime minister had reneged on a promise not to use the four day visit to advocate for the repatriation of the sculptures. Clearly this is a very sad situation between two NATO allies. The UK government argues that the sculptures were obtained legally and such an exchange would set a bad precedent that would undermine the collections of many of the world's major museums. The British have also argued that the British Museum offers a context for viewing the Elgin Marbles of other major ancient cultures.

The above shows how art provenance is an extremely difficult legal, moral, and ethical issue.

What would Ben Ferencz recommend?

One may only hypothesize.

Perhaps he would recommend and pursue the following. Given his huge contribution to the creation of the International Criminal Court he may recommend that the International Court of Arbitration (ICC) resolve this and all the other very similar disputes. 2023 was the centenary of the ICC, founded in 1923. The ICC has been at the forefront of supporting global trade and investment through dispute prevention and resolution. The ICC is based on the key principles that Ben Ferencz upheld, access to justice and the rule of law in the international dispute arena. The leaders of the movement that founded the ICC were called the "Merchants of Peace", as they believed fervently in the concept of trade, industry and commerce binding nations together, making individual nations prosperous and, most important and in alignment with Ben Ferencz's philosophy, less likely to resort to war if bound by mutual prosperity and strong trade relations. The ICC Court of Commercial Arbitration was inaugurated on January 19, 1923. Its history since has been prodigious, with in 2022 a milestone number of cases heard, with the 27,000[th] case being heard.

In 2023 the ICC issued a Centenary "Declaration on Dispute Prevention and Resolution", a visionary approach for dispute resolution and prevention for the 21st century. The high quality of ICC court members would meet with Ben Ferencz's approval. The above may be a positive and independent way ahead for art provenance resolution, all in the pursuit of peace.

EPILOGUE

The world has witnessed enormous stress and challenges since the Russian invasion of Ukraine in February, 2022. The second anniversary of that conflict approaches at the time of writing. Compounding this conflict was the October 7, 2022 attack on Israel by Hamas and the commencement of the most appalling loss of civilian lives in Gaza, innocent men, women, and children. The United Nations and Palestinian officials have estimated the losses in the thousands, as much as 20,000 plus at the time of writing, an appalling number. This number will most likely increase. It is salutary to look back and recall the Nazi inflicted deaths on the Jews, and in particular the trials of the Einsatzgruppen leadership that Ben Ferencz led as the prosecutor at the Nuremberg War Crimes Trials. It may seem inconceivable that in the 2020s the world is still experiencing such horrendous events, compounded by several more atrocities in various parts of Africa. In an era when adults in the democratic nations of the world seek peace and well being for their families and the older generation with grandchildren and great grandchildren want nothing but peace and serenity for their heirs and successors it is imperative to look back and see how lessons from the past dovetail with today's world, and how the work of people like Ben Ferencz, Claude Riley, and art may play in keeping the world safe, and at peace. "Peace in our Time" developed a negative cachet after Neville Chamberlain's ill fated agreement with Adolf Hitler in Munich. Chamberlain, Prime Minister of the United Kingdom May, 1937 to May, 1940, signed the Munich agreement with Hitler on September 30, 1938, ceding the German-speaking Sudetenland region of Czechoslovakia to Nazi Germany and Adolph Hitler. He was to realize very quickly that Hitler was not a man of his word. The Invasion of Poland by Nazi Germany followed between September 1, 1939-October 6, 1939, leading to World War Two.

Today the world faces a whole different set of challenges not just between Russia and Ukraine and Israel and Hamas and its surrogates. China and the Taiwan issue loom large. Iran and North Korea pose complex dangers to the democratic world, and terrorism has not gone away, reinvented constantly in different forms. The Houthis in Yemen pose a major threat, a proxy group for Iran that threatens peace and stability across both the Red Sea and on land against Saudi Arabia. Recent attacks on merchant shipping in the Red Sea by Houthis using drones and missiles highlights the threat to seaborne trade. The United States Navy has been proactive in maintaining the freedom of the seas and the rights of innocent passage by defeating such attacks. How may we progress, pursue Peace, and keep the world safe from the very worst possibility, nuclear warfare, with shades of the 1957 novel, "On the Beach" by the British-Australian author, Nevil Shute. Ben Ferencz would most certainly advocate a far more robust international legal architecture beyond institutions such as the International Court of Arbitration and the International Criminal Court. The veto power within the United Nations Security Council is an issue that needs to be addressed when various proactive peacekeeping measures run counter to the national self interests of countries such as China and Russia, both members of the United Nations Security Council. Violations by China of sovereign territory in East Asia is rife, with transgressions against for example the fishing rights within the 200 mile economic zone of the Philippines, Vietnam, and other nations. The United Nations Convention on the Law of the Sea (UNCLOS) specifically protects such vital national economic interests, along with other critical ocean related aspects, such as the rights of passage. Even though the International Court of Arbitration ruled against China for the seizure of key islands in the South China Sea, China forged ahead against international law and militarized the Spratley and Paracel Islands, created missile sites and other military installations. China then claimed the economic zones around these islands. Oil resources in the South China Sea may also have been a factor in China's seizures, along with the need to create offshore military bases on these islands. As a member of the Security Council China can veto measures aimed directly against illegal Chinese actions in the South China Sea. The United Nations Convention on the Law of the Sea (UNCLOS) needs greater enforcement mechanisms. The situation in the Red Sea emphasizes the criticality of shipping internationally and the types of threats posed by organizations such as the Houthis. Freedom of the seas is absolutely critical to world economic prosperity, indeed survival. On any given day it is estimated that more than $100 billion worth of trade is moving across the world's oceans. The Red Sea and the Babel Mandeb strait at the southern end of the Red Sea witness about 17,000 ship transits annually, with about 6.2 million barrels of oil transiting daily. The United States Navy is currently leading in protecting this area and making it clear to the world that Freedom of the Seas will be maintained. How a threat from an organization such as the Houthi can be addressed in terms of international law with clear and unequivocal enforcement mechanisms will be addressed shortly in the wider context of war crimes and crimes against humanity. The history of post World War Two Crimes against Humanity and War Crimes is a sad indictment on the international community for failure to constrain and indeed punish such actions. Even the leader of the world's democracies, the United States, is not totally innocent of such actions. The passing of the American statesman, Henry Kissinger, at age 100, brought into focus old controversies regarding US military actions in Cambodia during the Vietnam war. Media reports showed that the secret "Carpet Bombing" of Cambodia during the Vietnam War was kept from the American public. It is estimated that as many as 150,000 Cambodian civilians were killed in the B-52 saturation bombings authorized by Henry Kissinger, the National Security Adviser in the Nixon Administration. He argued that the attacks were strategic in nature, aimed at undermining North Vietnam's use of Cambodia as a way into South Vietnam. Was this a war crime? International lawyers may argue that deliberate attacks on civilian targets of the magnitude that occurred in Cambodia constitute a war crime. How to deter and prevent such war crimes and crimes against humanity in the future raises critical questions about the very nature and workings of the current international legal system, centered in The Hague, in the Netherlands. The number of regional and local conflicts ongoing in the world today present a daunting challenge against the backdrop of the current international legal and enforcement system. An authoritative new study finds that there are 183 regional and local conflicts ongoing at the time of writing. This is the highest number in three decades. The number is derived from an IISS survey (International Institute for Strategic Studies, based in London). The data was presented in the latest IISS annual "Armed Conflict Survey". It is not just Ukraine and the tragic situations in Gaza that have to be addressed.

The resolution of these conflicts is paramount for world peace.

The IISS survey concluded that for example in Ukraine's case only "Obtaining security guarantees that ensure Ukraine's future territorial integrity against external aggression" will lead to peace. The ending of the Gaza conflict is intensely complex. Together with for just a few examples in Azerbaijan (100,000 of its Armenian inhabitants fled the country), tensions between Russia and Georgia, between Algeria and Morocco, and in Pakistan domestic terrorism has worsened, and in India there are serious signs of major stresses regarding the anti-Muslim actions of the ruling Indian government. The International Committee of the Red Cross is a reliable supplier of data on global conflicts. The Committee currently catalogues 459 armed groups that present major humanitarian concerns. The Committee estimates that 195 million people may be living under either the direct or partial control of these armed groups. Within the United Nations key members present problems: China, Russia, Iran, North

Korea, Turkey, and the Gulf States – the democratic countries within the United Nations see these nations as representing and supporting authoritarian regimes. They disregard the fundamental principles enshrined since World War Two of international humanitarian law, the laws of war and war crimes, and the United Nations Convention on the Law of the Sea. Within Saudi Arabia it is recognized that various cruelties have become institutionalized. Mexico witnesses regular violence where organized crime and drug trafficking is a way of life. In Syria the survival of the tyrant Bashir al-Assad has been underwritten by Russian support, and Iraq continues to be torn by Sunni-Shiite Muslim divisions. Brazil, Myanmar, Nigeria, Somalia, and Afghanistan join a long list of countries fraught with internal dissent and violence. The effectiveness of United Nations peace keeping forces throughout the world has to be addressed. Over 70,000 United Nations forces are in conflict zones, wearing the blue berets of UN. They have been mostly in Africa, and the Middle East, especially South Sudan and the Central African Republic. UN peacekeepers have been deployed for decades in Cyprus and Southern Lebanon. Many UN peacekeepers have been killed while serving in threat intensive areas. For example, in Mali jihadist have killed 300 UN peacekeepers over a decade. This tragic situation is compounded by the veto using authoritarian states on the UN Security Council, with often mercenaries from these countries adding to the carnage in many of the states described above.

What then is the way ahead? What would Ben Ferencz recommend and lead if he was in charge today, given the ambivalent situation in the United Nations Security Council? Perhaps one aspect needs to be stressed before addressing Ben's likely policies. The United Nations General Assembly, together with its extensive staff and multitude of various institutions that operate within the United Nations, offers an alternate to the power wielded by the United Nations Security Council. The December, 2023 vote within the General Assembly calling for a ceasefire in Gaza shows the potential for change. A total of 153 countries voted for a ceasefire with only 10 member states, including the United States, voting against the resolution.

The title of the December 12, 2023 resolution is in itself significant: "Protection of civilians and upholding legal and humanitarian obligations". Ben Ferencz would have approved wholeheartedly of both the resolution and the outcome of the vote. What Ben Ferencz may have recommended today to strengthen the global response may look like this. The current two United Nations High Commissioners for Refugees and Human Rights would be expanded with the addition of a new separate, large, and strong United Nations High Commissioner for War Crimes and Crimes against Humanity. There would be a UN headquarters staff in New York and an equally significant High Commission staff associated with the International Criminal Court in The Hague. In both locations there would be a significant investigation staff operating across the globe. The staffs in both locations would be recruited from experienced law enforcement staffs from United Nations member states, augmented by a cadre of international lawyers well trained and experienced in matters relating to war crimes and crimes against humanity. Ben Ferencz would want the writ of the United Nations High Commission on War Crimes and Crimes against Humanity to operate globally. He would recognize that certain nations will oppose both the proposed structure and certainly the operation of investigatory staff in their territories. He would see this as inevitable in offending countries. However, he would recognize that there is deterrent value in such countries, particularly when leaders of such crimes wish to travel overseas or use ill gotten funds through the international banking system. A significant component of the investigatory arm of the new High Commission's organization would be a cadre of experienced intelligence personnel, exploiting in several domains the benefits of the digital revolution, particularly the use of Quantum computing technology and various applications of Artificial Intelligence. In addition Ben Ferencz would recognize the value of INTERPOL (the International Criminal Police Organization, with 196 member countries), and that the General Secretary and staff of INTERPOL would work in close association with the High Commission staff in both The Hague and New York. Key staff of the new High

Commission could be recruited from the intelligence communities of member states that show strong support for the new High Commission. Ben Ferencz spent decades working towards the creation of the International Criminal Court. What is described above would be a natural extension of all that he represented as both a fine lawyer, also a great human being. The pursuit of peace can never let up. All means have to be used to ensure the survival of our world, one that has become an increasingly challenging place for our children and grandchildren. Ben Ferencz would want no less than to implement change within the United Nations and to ensure that his quest for peace and justice endures.

Wisdom, Goodness, and Justice have to prevail over tyranny and dictatorship.

Let the spirit and legacy of Ben Ferencz prevail.

APPENDIX A

CURRENT AND EMERGING THREATS

The growing power of China and the development of what is clearly a "Grand Maritime Strategy" will play out in support of not just China's Belt and Road policy also China's overall strategic national security goals. This will affect not just US-UK Intelligence and the Five Eyes Intelligence community as a whole but increasingly their unilateral, bilateral, and multilateral relations with India, a crucial nation in the Indo-Pacific region. China's key policy statement issued in July 2019, "In the New Era" (issued by the State Council Information Office of the People's Republic of China) makes it abundantly clear where China is headed, with the Chinese Navy becoming the centerpiece and instrument of China's power and influence.

Insider Threats:

The years since 9/11 have seen the development of "insider threats" to not just the United States, the United Kingdom, and their allies, also all the main democratic nations in the West. This has come through the march of technology and for which new paradigms and technologies will be required in the post-2024 period to counter those who wish to penetrate the daily lives of individuals, businesses, and governments by electronic means. However, there is also the enduring factor of the more traditional insider threat posed by classical traitors and spies, and also those who betray sensitive and classified information in the name of the public good, and the protection of privacy.

New forms of propaganda, subliminal opinion forming, and disinformation are now commonplace in the digital era when so much information can be accumulated by the very nature of the internet and its vast information gathering capabilities. The large internet providers' huge data collection engines, analysis and storage capacity know as much about each individual subscriber, user, or customer as the governments of the countries in which they are located. Advertising and commercial transactions are drivers and the offshoots of this massive amount of data. The concept of privacy is moot when all of us as individuals make daily selections on the internet for news, products, and information searches that both define us and characterize our needs, likes, and dislikes. We are then naturally targeted by commercial entities, having provided a very detailed profile of our lifestyles, likes and dislikes at myriad different levels, including political persuasion. Classic spies gave away highly classified information on UK–US intelligence operations and personnel. Some gave away valuable technical information. The British GCHQ spy Geoffrey Prime was not unlike the Walkers in the United States, giving away extremely sensitive Navy operational and technical intelligence. Prime betrayed data on UK–US efforts to track Soviet strategic submarines, and various means by which the US Navy and Royal Navy used SIGINT and SOSUS. 1985 became the "Year of the Spy" in the United States. Ronald Pelton was exposed at the National Security Agency; the Walker spy ring was broken up; at the CIA Edward Lee Howard was caught spying, and in November 1985 Jonathan Pollard was arrested for spying for the Israeli Mossad. After 1985 Aldrich Ames was exposed at the CIA, and Robert Hanssen at the FBI, both giving critical information on CIA HUMINT operations and counterintelligence operations to the Soviet Union. Much later the case of Edward Snowden, who copied and leaked classified information from NSA. He did this, so he claimed, in the name of "Liberty versus Security," exposing several key global surveillance programs run by NSA and the Five Eyes, with cooperation from various telecommunications companies and European governments. Many of these spies' modus operandi could have been penetrated not by just better physical security checks and vetting procedures, in addition to covert review of bank accounts and personal communications, but also and very importantly by better and sophisticated monitoring of access to computer data. There are very good tools available with real-time checks for not just regular access to sensitive data, but unwarranted and out-of-hours computer access, and certainly the removal of data via a thumb drive, disc, and hard copy printer and reproduction. Programs can immediately alert security personnel to unusual and or out of routine access. For example, anyone accessing US-UK Intelligence data using a thumb drive should sound an alarm immediately if there is no prior approval for such action. The current threat situation in 2024 is more insidious than the above type of espionage threats. The internet poses the greatest challenge to US-UK Intelligence since the dawn of SIGINT. The cooperation of the Five Eyes and their trusted allies in a concerted technical and operational effort to develop new ways to cope with the overwhelming amount of data transmitted every millisecond on the internet is paramount. No one country can claim dominance and certainly all the brain power and skills of New Zealand, Canada, Australia, the UK, and the US are required. Cyber-attacks have and will continue to take multiple forms. Long before the current wave of cyber-attacks there had been, for example in the 1990s, attacks on the New Zealand power grid in Auckland and the London banking system. In parallel, companies began to provide privacy protection via encryption technologies fairly early on. The renowned PEP (Pretty Good Privacy) 1993 case in the United States is an exemplar of the march of commercial innovation that complicated Five Eyes' SIGINT operations. The American Phil Zimmermann provided the public worldwide with "Public Key Cryptography," and the case against him by the US government failed miserably. As the British government was investing in building the "Doughnut" to house GCHQ in the late 1990s, at the time the largest construction program in both the UK and Europe, both GCHQ and NSA were increasingly facing the daunting challenge of intercepting unprecedented volumes of data that even with the most advanced "keyword" searches could not keep up in situations where, for example, likely targets were using coded words in Pashtu, Farsi, and multiple obscure dialects, making life extremely challenging for the dedicated Five Eyes listeners and analysts. Traffic analysis became the order of the day as a quick and easy way to attempt to isolate threat data. In light of this observation it becomes clear that the US and UK governments, in their urgent need to protect their citizens and those of their closest allies from burgeoning terrorism, faced the challenge of "Liberty versus Security," in the vernacular of the debate over the mass trawling of personal data from the internet and phone calls. In retrospect it is very easy to discern that the US and UK were up against intractable odds, with terrorist groups changing their cell phones and SIM cards regularly, often every few days, and transmitting in worded codes and dialects. At the operational intelligence level in the field these challenges were faced over time very effectively by robust and highly intelligent tactical SIGINT systems, such as those used in Afghanistan. None of these systems depended on NSA- or GCHQ-derived data, unlike, for example, in earlier years when United States Air Force targets against Serbia were derived directly from GCHQ and NSA data. There was no highly reliable SIGINT that, for example, confirmed or denied the existence, location, and possible types of WMD in Iraq in 2003. The head of the United Nations investigative team in Iraq, Hans Blix, kept his team on the ball looking for hidden WMD. Data mining and using "Voice Prints" or the recordings of likely suspects for matching with vast amounts of intercepted communications were still in their infancy. Drone technology was barely off the ground in 2003. In fact, as late as 2010 countries such as the UK did not have any effective drones for surveillance and reconnaissance. All this has changed rapidly with the Ukraine war witnessing the unprecedented use of drone technology. Computer Innovations and their Impact on Intelligence: The revolutionary Cray supercomputers1 first designed in 1972 by Seymour Cray were subsequently supplanted by a series of massive parallel computers built by a large number of companies in the 1980s. However, by 2000 Cray was the only remaining supercomputing provider in the Western market, with its one rival, NEC Corporation. Ordinary mainframe computers were still very much the order of the day at most large corporate and US-UK intelligence centers. Cray went into Chapter 11 bankruptcy in March 1995, and in February 1996 Cray Research merged with Silicon Graphics (SGI). SGI's Cray Research Business Unit was subsequently sold to Tera Computing Company in March 2000. In April 2008 Cray and Intel joined to collaborate on future computing systems. By 2009 they produced the fastest computer in the world for the National Center for Computational Sciences at the Oak Ridge National Laboratories. Fast forwarding to October 2017 Cray, together with partner Microsoft Azure, brought supercomputing to "the cloud," and in the same year built two new Cray CS-Storm systems for artificial intelligence workloads and on April 18, 2018, Cray announced the development of the most advanced processors to the Cray CS500 product line. Cray continues to make more revolutionary advances. The 2020s will witness limitless advances that will make the great innovations of the 1970–2000 timeframe seem like computing dinosaurs. By its very nature, the US and the UK and their Five Eyes partners from the turn of the century onwards have faced an uphill battle of keeping up with the march of technology. Private commercial companies have been far ahead of the UK–US governments in innovation and introduction to the commercial marketplace. A company such as Google is ahead of the game compared with NSA, GCHQ, and the Canadian, Australian, and New Zealand equivalents. Part of the problem is the very nature of the acquisition and contracting culture, particularly in the UK and

US, with regimes that are slow and ponderous and not quick to adjust to changing technological circumstances. Added to this procurement plight is the inability to deal with vibrant and innovative startups with often critical disruptive technology that may challenge the secure multi-year contracts of large companies whose products are, in effect, already obsolete. This critical problem will have to be faced by the US and the UK, and in particulate the United States Departments of Defense and Homeland Security, plus their intelligence agencies, as the 2020s progress. On Thursday, July 7, 2005 the UK had its tragic and devastating wake up call, with the suicide bomber attacks in central London. This was the deadliest attack on British soil, and by British nationals, since World War II. This presented GCHQ with the need to rethink its total surveillance strategy. The worrisome thing is that between 2005 and today the pace and scale of technological change has been greater than could ever have been anticipated. The ability to process data has to be accompanied by advanced decision aids that convert vast amounts of information to relatively tiny amounts of critically important actionable intelligence that will enable decision makers to be ahead of the threat.

Intelligence and Drugs:

There is a heroin–opioid epidemic in the United States, and to a lesser extent in The UK. Heroin is a highly addictive drug processed from morphine, a naturally occurring substance from the seed pod of poppy plant varieties. When sold as a drug it appears as a white or brownish powder. Opium is refined to make morphine, and then further refined, with various additives (some extraordinarily destructive to the body) into different forms of "street heroin." Opioids act on the human opioid receptors and have similar effects to morphine, in essence pain killers. Opioids have legitimate medical applications regularly prescribed by medical practitioners. Some experts claim that less professional practitioners either overprescribe or unnecessarily prescribe opioids instead of using other therapies— the pill-popping syndrome. Used non-medically without proper control they produce euphoric effects like an illegal drug. Excessive use leads to dependence, withdrawal symptoms and, particularly when combined with other depressant drugs, results in death from respiratory failure. By 2020 a combination of recreational use, addiction, and over prescription, plus illicit inexpensive heroin, has led to millions of Americans, young and old, dependent and dying in large numbers. Narcan is the brand name for "Naloxone," and is used medically, indeed it is vital for paramedics in US rescue squads, to block the effects of opioid overdose. Rescue for paramedics in US rescue squads, to block the effects of opioid overdose. Rescue squads and emergency rooms administer intravenously and by injection. Often multiple doses are required to save the patient. If a US rescue squad runs out of Narcan this becomes a critical situation for a patient in need of urgent life support. By the time a unit arrives at an emergency room it may be too late. In the US, West Virginia, for example, has a nationally excessively high addiction rate. West Virginia rescue squad units often have to attend the same victims, indeed whole families, on more than one occasion during a 24-hour period. The overall impact of this is not good if rescue units are not available for trauma cases (traffic accidents and so on) and medical emergencies (heart attack, stroke, emergency childbirth and so on). Heroin arrives in the US and the other nations via a discreet distribution chain. Breaking that chain and arresting the criminals who make millions at the top end of this chain, and more modest sums at the bottom ends, and preventing distribution to our vulnerable fellow citizens, are clear US-UK operational intelligence objectives. The drug cartels that manage and operate the initial distribution depend on international shipping, in addition to the fast speed Caribbean shipments and small submarine operations that have been documented in the media. US-UK tracking of drug shipments requires multi-intelligence sources and methods. This tracking of rogue ships is not new to US-UK Intelligence. Each of the nations contribute to a 24/7 global tracking network relying on satellite intercepts, SIGINT, AIS (Automatic Identification System)-related data, and key HUMINT at places such as production sites and ports of embarkation. The heroin routes can be monitored from poppy fields to port delivery. Drug forensics permit obtaining the details of specific batches of the heroin's origin. Breaking into the money chain is as important as tracking illicit international shipping. The laundering of international drug money requires intensive analysis of offshore accounts, covert cover up schemes to hide drug operations and payments and at the lower level the ways and means by which drug pusher suspects' financials can be accessed. This requires the most intensive US-UK cooperation from ship tracking to financial analysis. Coastguards, or their equivalents, are important in the final stages of ship transits once vessels enter

territorial waters, to board and search suspect vessels. The US Coast Guard Foundation Calendar states: "Every day the Coast Guard screens an average of 360 merchant ships for potential risks before they arrive in US ports," and: "Each day, vigilant Coast Guard patrols prevent over 1,000 pounds of illegal drugs from reaching our communities." In international waters the navies of the US and the UK, their Five Eyes partners, and their close allies can legally board and search suspect vessels. The additive materials used in the manufacture of heroin, particularly the more virulent varieties, are well known and their manufacture and distribution to locations where the "mixing" takes place can be traced. This process requires the involvement of multiple national agencies beside the traditional intelligence agencies of US-UK Intelligence. In tracking heroin from poppy fields to street "pushers" requires drug enforcement agencies, local and federal/central government law enforcement agencies, sheriff departments, and customs authorities. The law enforcement task is further complicated by heroin distribution via mail, as opposed to by hand. Data "Fusion Centers" that combine the resources of both the intelligence agencies and law enforcement agencies at all levels (federal/government to local) with specialist drug enforcement agencies are crucial in the fight against heroin and other drugs' distribution. The same problems exist with breaking into drug cartels' communications that exist with terrorist organizations where awareness has made the bad guys much more resilient and cunning in their communications' evasion and deception techniques If there was one single weak point in the distribution chain it is in the shipping/ transport process, whatever form that takes. The big cartels want to make major shipments, not dribs and drabs over protracted periods, because of the loss of revenue. Shipment delays to avoid and confuse interception require more complex planning and execution. A chain with a weak link is vulnerable, and as the 2020s progress more and more effort will be required in this interception phase based on good intelligence of the total system, not just one part. Knowledge of where and when shipments will be made, and their ports of embarkation, are crucial data points. Corruption will be an ongoing problem, particularly in the law enforcement side of counter drug operations. The best US-UK intelligence can be thwarted by corrupt law enforcement and customs officials turning a blind eye to shipments and distribution. This will continue to require stricter vetting procedures and in the case of discreet high-level classified intelligence, restricting access not only to limited need-to-know personnel, but also providing the type of computer and data security discussed earlier. In the digital era it is possible to not just restrict access but to know what, when, and how each individual had access to data, and what uses were made of data. Counterintelligence can focus quite intensively on data paths and usage, particularly timing and other associations with highly specific data sets. Artificial intelligence techniques combined with, for example, advanced Bayesian mathematics employing the most sophisticated log likelihood theory applications, can be used to analyze large real-time intelligence data sets in ways that were impossible for individual analysts striving to not just make sense of massive amounts of data, but deliver answers for users in very constrained time lines. Today relatively simple AI applications can make the intelligence analyst's job faster, less stressful, and vitally more productive. AI can quickly visually recognize people across international boundaries, recognize speech, and instantly translate the most daunting languages and dialects, while executing sophisticated tasks allied to machines processing data from a vast amount of accumulated experience and learning built into the AI systems that will then adjust to new changing inputs in or near real time. Machines can therefore demonstrate intelligence when the computer copies or mimics human cognitive functions that we all normally associate with how we learn and solve problems. The evolutionary algorithms are however created by human beings, not in any way self-generated by the machine, a popular misconception. If the machine and the operator can work together as if the machine is another human being then the machine has passed the "Turing Test" developed by the famous Bletchley Park code breaker Alan Turing in 1950. AI is progressing by leaps and bounds and will undoubtedly add an extraordinary dimension to US-UK Intelligence, which at the time of writing in 2024 is almost impossible to predict. One fact does undoubtedly remain. Alan Turing was a genius. US-UK Intelligence requires more like him to revolutionize the intelligence process. Finding them is the challenge but they are out there in the bright new generation of computer scientists and mathematicians.

Global Terrorism, Human Trafficking, Piracy, Illicit Arms Transfers and Money Laundering: Global terrorism, human trafficking, piracy, gun running, illicit arms transfers, and the associated money laundering with these activities, have ushered in new challenges for US-UK Intelligence, not dissimilar to international drug trafficking. The common thread that runs through all these operations is money. They all require the acquisition, transfer, and dispersal of funds in order to function. "Following the money" is an appropriate adage. The other common thread, with the possible exception of human trafficking, is weaponry. Weapons are required in order for these operations to function. Money and weapons are the lifeblood of these evil activities. Preventing and or disrupting the flow is a key goal. A multi-source intelligence approach is required. Added to this mix is the crucial task of locating and tracking the means and methods of transnational recruitment and training, particularly in the terrorist domain, and in those other domains that are more of an international criminal nature where individuals are lured in, corrupted, or wittingly join the ranks, trained, and paid for their wrongdoing. The means are as important therefore as the individuals and knowing the nature and dimensions of these means is paramount for successful intelligence operations in the future.

Since 9/11, cooperation has been the order of the day. Long gone are the days when, for instance, in the 1980s an NSA Director, Lieutenant General William Odom, US Army, decided to cut off NSA intelligence flow to New Zealand because of New Zealand's ban on US nuclear warships and submarines entering New Zealand ports. This was short lived, with GCHQ and the Australians supplying the New Zealand GCSB (Government Communications Security Bureau) with SIGINT and other intelligence. In fact, NSA working personnel surreptitiously worked around Odom's ban, such is the core strength and relationships within the Five Eyes. Nothing in the future, and particularly the whims and fancies of political change within each of the Five member states, should jeopardize the continuum of Five Eyes 24/7 working cooperation. Arms dealers and the middlemen, who operate in the shadows, often acting sub rosa for governments, are key targets since they mastermind the deals and transfers of funds to those who provide and those who receive weapons. Israel's operations and arms deals with Russia and Iran, in light of contemporary international relations, are eye openers. What they provide is a template for thwarting arms deals that are clearly and unambiguously dangerous for the global order. This requires close collaboration rather than unilateral dealings. The sort of operations that CIA officers such as the legendary, perhaps infamous, James Jesus Angleton (1917–1987) ran at the CIA in the early Cold War decades with little or no cooperation with the other Five Eyes, is perhaps an object lesson in how to both create a certain amount of chaos but more important seriously jeopardize the joint collection, analysis, and sharing of Five Eyes intelligence. The key motivation driving both illicit and clandestine arms deals and the appalling consequences of human trafficking is money. However, out-of-control covert intelligence operations without proper oversight can and has led to disastrous political repercussions. The Iran–Contra affair illustrates this well. The intersection of intelligence as an arm of political policy is clearly a most troubling scenario. As the 2020s progress the US and the UK together with the other three Five Eyes will have to pool their total resources. Based on a complete review of stand-alone clandestine intelligence operations since 1947 by the United States, it is recommended that unless there are overwhelming reasons for a stand-alone US covert intelligence operation, then the Five Eyes should work together in collaboratively tracking money, people, and weapons. This covers not only 24/7 electronic and other means of exchanging data, but the constant interaction of Five Eyes personnel not just through the various personnel exchange programs but through constant meetings. The March 11, 2004 Atocha railway station bombings in Madrid, Spain, with 192 killed and approximately 2000 people injured, showed that in tracking the al-Qaeda terrorist cell involved there had been insufficient close working relations between the various European intelligence and law enforcement agencies. The bombings were the deadliest terrorist attacks carried out in the history of Spain and Western Europe. Close working-level meetings between the agencies may well have improved considerably the Spanish understanding and interpretation of the available intelligence data. As the 2020s progress more and more close working meetings will be required to address not just weapon and human trafficking, but also the wider strategic intelligence issues. The end games for both illicit and illegal arms deals, weapons movements and human trafficking are well understood—the motivation, the locations, the customers, and the likely possible routes. Take for example the AR-15 and AK-47 Kalashnikov weapons that are used extensively on the global markets, both legally and illegally. Like almost every weapon, including those weapons that are manufactured ostensibly for official government military purposes, US-UK Intelligence knows where they are manufactured, both overtly and covertly. Tracking their sale and distribution is an art and a science of modern intelligence operations. The political context is the art, and the science involves the myriad technical intelligence sources and methods to track their movements and end users. Large weapons present an easier profile—tanks and armored personnel carriers are easier to track than Uzi submachine guns or RPGs (rocket propelled grenades). Part of the problem is that nation states indulge in clandestine arms deals. Corrupt money deals often underlay the reasons for purchase, with paybacks for the key top people in the process, with hard cash passing between the principals, not via international banking. International relationships are not always what they appear to be. Today it may seem a total disconnect that major Western European countries and Israel were major arms suppliers to Iran, and that countries that could not necessarily go direct to the arms manufacturer or middlemen would use surrogates. In the early days of the Cold War, Israel was a major source of intelligence on the Soviet Union because of the large number of Jews still in Russia and other Soviet states, and the backwards and forwards of Russian Jews, while at the same time that Israel was collecting intelligence it was also buying arms from eastern bloc sources, particularly Czechoslovakia, with the full knowledge of their Soviet masters. This apparent symbiosis is likely to continue, and US-UK Intelligence will have to not just work much more closely together in tracking and inhibiting weapon and human trafficking, they will have to be open about mutual political agendas. Outstanding intelligence organizations are communities of very talented and mostly hugely ethical people serving common purposes of protecting critical national interests. The United States in particular may have to adjust some of its modus operandi in terms of greater transparency and sharing, though all under total security. Money laundering tends to accompany terrorist weapons and explosives purchases, drug cartels, human trafficking, piracy financials, and gun running, together with more opaque weapons procurements. The technological edge can defeat these operations. In addition to the types of technologies that we have already discussed, new technologies will augment the massive search and analysis engines being developed for both GCHQ and NSA, with technology sharing with the Canadians, the Australians, and New Zealanders. Two examples will suffice: artificial intelligence (AI) can add to the sources and methods mix in hitherto unexplored domains, particularly when using a holistic approach to say gun running and arms transfers with very clever cognitive tools, that will automatically provide the sort of warnings and indicators that lead to interception, arrest, and seizure. Similarly, shared drone technology will enhance Five Eyes surveillance with stealth, improved power to density propulsion systems that will extend range and endurance, and ever-increasing sophisticated SIGINT and IMINT payloads with real time low probability of intercept data links. These new techniques will be added to the classical armory of SIGINT, IMINT, HUMINT, GEOINT, ACINT, and MASINT in all their myriad forms, and used in a fully integrated way so that the speed and accuracy of initial detection and location are enhanced. Drones are here to stay. The Ukraine war has made this manifest. The more sophisticated stealthy covert drones with long endurance and highly capable sensors will augment the more lightweight tactical drones in adding to the SIGINT, ELINT, ELECTRO-OPINT/INFRA-RED, and IMINT capabilities of airborne and space systems, whose whereabouts are often known by the threat. Drones are very versatile, and in money terms, hugely cost effective. They can be launched from ships and submarines, from friendly territories using surrogates, and not so friendly nations clandestinely. They can self-destruct in the worst scenarios. Locating and tracking portside activities using drones can become both more efficient and less risky than employing covert human operatives. Paramount in this technological leap forward still remains the key collective strengths of the US and UK Intelligence, the Five Eyes as a whole and their key allies. In my 50 years of intelligence experience, there can be no hiding vital information that is of mutual benefit. For example, Canada may not have the same historic and current SIGINT organization of the British at GCHQ and the Americans at NSA, but the Canadians have a vast network through their embassies that augment their traditional CSE covert collection operations. The same applies to the Australians and New Zealanders. The sum of all parts will be more and more crucial as we move into the second quarter of the 21st century. The combined navies of the US and the UK and their allies represent a prodigious round-the-clock forward-deployed presence to counter the international trade in illicit arms. These navies are complemented by the navies of friendly and allied powers. The Five Eyes share data with and through the US National Maritime Intelligence Center (NMIC) and the associated echelons in the other four countries. Locating and tracking rogue ships transporting illicit arms is today a hallmark of the Five Eyes navies. For example:on March 28, 2016, USS Sirocco intercepted a dhow in the Arabian Sea and confiscated 1,500 AK-47s, 200 Arabian Sea and confiscated 1,500 AK-47s, 200 RPGs, and 21 .50 caliber machine guns (these are manufactured by several nations including the Russians and Chinese); on August 27, 2018, USS *Jason Dunham* tracked and intercepted a stateless dhow (not flying a national flag) in international waters in the Gulf of Aden off the coast of Yemen. Aerial surveillance showed the crew throwing packages of AK-47s into a skiff. The following day, August 28, 2018, USS *Jason Dunham* boarded and seized the weapons that included more than a 1000 AK-47s. The above illustrates countless at-sea operations. Five Eyes shared intelligence and cooperation with other friendly navies has paid serious dividends. Intelligence and the Middle East: Will the Past Be Prologue? It is not the purpose here to reexamine the intelligence failures that occurred prior to and after the invasion of Iraq. These issues have been addressed by many authors and much of the product is axiomatic. From a current threat perspective and a US-UK Intelligence perspective however there remains one key overriding issue. This is the separation of individual single state policy (that is the policies of the United States and the United Kingdom) from both individual state-sponsored intelligence collection and analysis from collective Five Eyes intelligence collection and analysis. This is an important issue and it involves total Five Eyes agreements and also the separate bi-lateral and multi-lateral intelligence agreements and intelligence exchanges that exist between the Five Eyes nations. The United States has, for example, pursued different policies in the Middle East than the other four nations, sometimes contentiously, with disagreement, as is clear from Five Eyes ambassadorial statements and votes in the United

Nations. As has been stated several times, intelligence products, particularly key assessments from the various Five Eyes Joint Intelligence Committees, or their equivalent, should not be subject to any form of political pressure or influence. Intelligence's role is to provide the highest quality unvarnished information for policy makers without any skewing of data to support either national policy or the political motives or intentions of political parties and national leadership. Intelligence should be at arms' length. It is never the role of intelligence to make policy. In this regard US-UK Intelligence and the Five Eyes therefore hold collectively the moral high ground. The intelligence agencies and departments of the Five Eyes have an ethical standard to maintain, insofar as they cannot be swayed in their assessments by political exigencies, notwithstanding that there may at times be disagreement or varying interpretations of intelligence data. The latter is a different issue, and can be a sign of a healthy, vibrant, and professional organization. As the 2020s progress it is crucial that the cohesiveness of US-UK Intelligence and the Five Eyes as a whole endures and adheres in spite of national political policy differences to the above ethical considerations. US-UK Intelligence has known one enduring fact since the 1950s, and the consequences of the 1967 June War that has led to many contentions ever since. This is the need for intelligence collectors and analysts to truly know and understand the Middle East in detail, from every dimension, and not just in terms of classical political and international relations and diplomacy as practiced in the West, but in terms of the deep history, culture, political origins and developments since World War II; religions, economies, educational systems, traditions, family structure and community organization; diverse languages and dialects, and the origins of current and likely future political alignments and intentions—both internally, regionally, and internationally. Without that knowledge and experience US-UK Intelligence can, potentially, be clutching at straws in spite of the very best intelligence collection systems. There has to be greater awareness of the various shifts in all these variables as many external international players, some at total odds with US-UK interests, seek to pursue their national self-interests in what is likely the most conflicted region in the world, and one from which can emit the worst of consequences. History and culture come together in abundant strength in the Middle East. Understanding these is a prerequisite. The aftermath of the occupation–invasion of Iraq in 2003 was clearly not adequately assessed prior to military operations, a huge lesson in itself. At the core of this issue most likely lay a fundamental lack of understanding of the history and culture of the Middle East. The latter were not fully understood and factored into decision making in the White House. Herewith lay a potential recipe for strategic disaster. We must have collective understanding not just of why we are where we are today in the Middle East, but also the systemic underpinnings that are driving regional politics in ways that no one in Washington would have predicted in 2001. Over the past twenty two years there have been many academic analyses and intelligence assessments regarding the rise of ISIS and its apparent successes. Interpretations have varied, in some cases quite significantly. Some researchers have attributed responsibility to Washington, while the others have seen al-Qaeda in Iraq (AQI) as the driving force behind the emergence and growth of ISIS. The overall fall-out of these varying views is that it is a far more difficult and complex process to comprehend what caused the emergence of ISIS in 2006 and its claims to be a state. Despite various US political pronouncements, ISIS today, in 2023, is far from eliminated. Although it has suffered serious military defeats and many of its leaders have been eliminated, it has a most unfortunate ability to regenerate and garner more supporters. ISIS has been declared defeated on several occasions only to reappear. The internet plays a role in the ISIS recruitment process and although US-UK Intelligence very successfully tracks much of this, there remains the challenge of countering the recruitment process, training, and the supply of weapons. Syria and Iraq lie at a geo-strategic crossroads, where the Sunni and the Shi'a worlds intersect. From the south to the north there is the main Sunni line, from the Gulf countries to Turkey. The Shi'a area stretches from the east to the west and consists primarily of Iran and Hezbollah. Syria and Iraq have mixed populations, and until the beginning of the 20th century both these countries had secular regimes, with mixed populations of Sunni and Shi'a communities coexisting in similar economic and sociopolitical conditions. The role of ideology and doctrine in the Middle East should never be underestimated. The struggle between Shi'a and Sunni Muslims has not ceased since the 7th century. The ruling regime, whether Sunni or Shi'a, is what determines outcomes, irrespective of population and Moslem demographics—Bahrain, for example, is a Sunni state, though it has a Shi'a majority. This key overlay should drive both intelligence collection and analysis. ISIS appeared just after the Iraq parliamentary elections of 2005, initially in January. The Shi'ites obtained the overwhelming majority in the National Assembly. In January 2005 the two main Shi'a parties obtained 180 seats (the Kurds receiving 75 seats, the rest, 20). These results led to a wave of criticism, and the elections were repeated. In spite of an increasing number of Sunni votes, the Shi'a United Iraqi Alliance got 128 seats out of 275 (Kurds 53, the Sunnis altogether 58). The civil war began, as the Sunni population would not acknowledge the legitimacy of the elections. The main role was played by terrorist groups that had evolved from breakup of the Iraqi army and what became AQI, and later ISIS. In June 2005 Washington began a "Together Forward" operation, which finished in October. Immediately after that, ISIS appeared. This precipitated a reaction by those in Iraq not disposed to the US occupation, uniting them in a common purpose, to challenge the United States. ISIS consisted of some elements of the terrorist groups defeated in the civil war, including AQI, and other subdivisions and generals of Saddam Hussein's army. Though distinct entities, these groups displayed similarities. They combined to fight a common enemy, the Americans, and their aim was to expel the US from Iraq. What is much more important to observe is that they are all Sunnis. The very name of a new group, Islamic State of Iraq, marked a key common and unifying claim: to create a Sunni state by a Sunni political elite. To ignore this crucial fact is to blindside Five Eyes intelligence operations and assessments. Sponsorship from the Gulf countries helped them to join together. ISIS's early emergence therefore is not directly related to the Washington government, to AQI, or to economic factors such as poverty, but rather support from the Gulf and, in particular, from Saudi Arabia and Qatar. Saudi Arabia has always claimed to be an indisputable leader between the Sunni communities, and is a Sunni regional leader. Although Qatar had intensified its connections with European countries in order to increase its GDP, Qatar still needed to have a Sunni key relationship to the north. Syria was ruled by the Alawi kin and showed political affinity for Iran, and Iraq had a strictly secular regime and a Shi'a majority in population. As a consequence, the Gulf countries such as Qatar felt a strong need for a separate Sunni state. If these fundamental facts are ignored it is clearly possible for US-UK Intelligence and the Five Eyes as a whole to go astray in making assessments. The First Gulf War, Iraq, August 1990: The invasion of Kuwait by Saddam Hussein, August 2–4, 1990, eliminated a chance for the US and its allies to cooperate with his regime, while good relations between the Assad family and the Iranian government opened the door to challenges to US influence. Readers should bear in mind one key aspect that a former head of the Israeli Mossad, Efraim Halevy, points out in his book, *Man in the Shadows*: "The beginning of our journey in this book took us to Baghdad and to the key player, Saddam Hussein—confronting the Shiite revolutionary hurricane emanating from Iran. Hussein was then the savior of the modern Arab world and the vital interests of the United States in the region." The tragic irony that the Mossad chief points out underscores a crucial fact that, much as Saddam Hussein was a well-proven extremely evil man in many ways, he was the regional bulwark against Iran and indeed the dire enemy of an emergent threat from al-Qaeda. Much earlier in his book Halevy points out that it was Saudi Arabia, not in any shape or form Iraq, that supported Moslem extremism and provided most of the manpower for the 9/11 attacks.8 Moderate Arab leaders had always indicated to the West that Hussein, bad person that he was, provided the best defense against both Iran and Islamic extremism. Halevy towards the end of his book makes a significant statement regarding WMD, and particularly the nuclear element, that Islamic extremists are much more likely to use WMD, including nuclear weapons, and by implication when revisiting his assessment of Hussein and Iraq, pose far more of a threat than ever Hussein did. Halevy shows how moderate and loyal allies of the West, such as King Hussein of Jordan, followed a position of neutrality and a tilt towards Iraq in 1991 and the First Gulf War because he realized that Saddam Hussein kept the region safe from Iranian intrusion and a Shi'ite resurgence. Halevy states regarding Hezbollah: "However, it has one more characteristic that distinguished it from Khammas and Al Qaeda: It is the Shiite movement allied with Iran … in these respects Hezbollah will have to renounce much more than Khammas if it wishes its dreams of respectability to come true."10 These quotes from a distinguished former Mossad chief show an analysis of the region that was tragically either forgotten, ignored, or never appreciated in the first instance, in the headlong haste to invade Iraq. After the invasion the political instability created in Iraq, particularly from 2006, allowed a Sunni organization with a clear political course to gain momentum towards, potentially, the creation of its own state. The Sunni state lying between the Gulf and Turkey had to facilitate laying a gas pipeline from Qatar to Europe and also divide the Shi'a geopolitical and theocratic space into two unconnected parts. This view of a new Sunni state also solved the Saudi problem of political leadership. Syria, primarily agrarian, and Iraq, an oil producer, would not challenge Saudi and Gulf state economic supremacy. It is important to recall that ISIS had been waiting near the Syrian–Iraqi borders and began its expansion in 2013–2014. Why did it wait so long to act? The answer is that ISIS could not establish itself solidly in the Sunni territories of Iraq, as it would have to face surrounding forces, both the Shi'as of southern Iraq and neighboring countries, and the Kurds. Also, it could not connect directly to Turkey, or any sea, so from a strategic viewpoint ISIS, while solely in Iraq, had strategic limitations. However, ISIS saw an opportunity in Syria. When the Western intervention in Syria began, after two years of civil war, when all conflicting parties and the population became exhausted, ISIS crossed the border and interfered in the war. ISIS needed support from the local population. The idea of a Caliphate was created in order to win over peoples in the newly controlled territories. Syria became therefore a critical factor in ISIS's survival and possible growth. In retrospect it is clear that the main aim of ISIS was in fact to establish a state, a serious challenge for the West, the region, and the US-UK intelligence apparatus, and one that had to be internally stable and could in fact be used by the Gulf countries as a bridge between them and the West. The early success of ISIS militarily can be explained not by military superiority but rather the total fatigue of Syria and Iraq caused by civil disorders and external intervention by Russia and the West, and occasional incursions by Israeli air strikes. However, this very scenario also militated in the other direction, preventing ISIS from gaining stable control in a hugely volatile environment that remains to this day. The chief political–military objective of the United States and the United Kingdom has been to contain and at best eliminate ISIS in Syria, while creating an environment in which the Assad regime will negotiate. The latter has been exacerbated by Russian support for the Assad regime and the very complexity of the ethnic–political–religious diversity that divides Syria. By the spring of 2019 ISIS had suffered major military defeats in Syria. The question remains about the future of the remaining ISIS fighters and their families and supporters in Syria. Will they disperse, and if so, where to? Will they be integrated? Will they be interned in camps? The situation is still ambivalent. Moreover, what will happen to the many foreign nationals who were fighting for the defeated ISIS in Syria? These people remain in transit. Will their countries of origin accept them back and attempt cultural rehabilitation? In some cases, countries of origin may charge returning ISIS fighters with terrorist offences. For those ISIS supporters who are not Syrian nationals what is their economic and social future? Time has shown too that ISIS regenerates. It is crucial, naturally, that this is not allowed to occur. Intelligence is crucial in this process of identifying where and how such regeneration is occurring. We know that the so-called "domestic" strategy of ISIS was centered on creating a state, a propagandist tool if unrealistic. ISIS has never tried to break into Shi'a territories, and in both Iraq and Syria they have claimed to want to control only Sunni lands. They have, however, tried to capture some parts of Kurdistan in order to reach the Turkish border. ISIS's direct territorial control strategy, most likely a pipe-dream, appears to have been the basis for developing a caliphate ideology that would allow Syrians and Iraqis to tolerate their loss of sovereignty and influence, by creating a theocratic self-identity as an Umar-like11 caliphate. Fortunately, none of this has been achieved, while the current situation in Syria remains volatile, unpredictable, with massive dislocation, intense suffering, and a massive refugee problem for Jordan in particular. From an intelligence perspective it is important to place ISIS within the much bigger Islamic framework outside of current state structures. ISIS has been criticized severely for direct violations of sharia law by various groups within Islam. However, none of the key theologians or religious leaders have dared as yet to publish fatwa against the ISIS regime. The Moslem intelligentsia, within the religious leadership, has come out in direct criticism in light of ISIS atrocities of massive proportions. The latter has been exemplified by the violent treatment of non-Muslim women. Intelligence can provide data that will show how to ideologically target those populations and communities most vulnerable to ISIS recruitment propaganda by using well-constructed counter propaganda, employing all the subtleties of dialect and local culture. Prior to the mid-2010s ISIS could claim some success by creating state-like institutions. The ISIS regime has provided in areas where they have or had control electricity, water, and facilitated building schools and hospitals, roads, and mosques. US-UK Intelligence collection has and remains important in the ways in which ISIS seeks to control perception of itself, and especially where ISIS wishes to be perceived by the local populations as an organization that tends to do best for its people. ISIS would like to have itself perceived by its grass-roots followers, and those who are caught innocently in the turmoil of theocratic cross-fire, as the political conjunction of the material and spiritual, in fulfillment of its people's needs for stability. As the 2020s progress the US and the UK in particular will need to exploit more effectively ISIS technical and theocratic vulnerabilities in coercing populations and particularly paramilitary recruits to its ranks. There is a requirement for a more sophisticated approach to media interactions by US-UK Intelligence, far more capable than for example "The Voice of America" during the Cold War.

There is a requirement for a more sophisticated approach to media interactions by US-UK Intelligence, far more capable than for example "The Voice of America" during the Cold War. As we observed above, dealing with ISIS propaganda and recruitment requires detailed sophisticated insight into local cultures and dialects. One key ISIS vulnerability is open to penetration: the reality and the perception that ISIS has spiraled into atrocity after atrocity, driven by an evil creed of violence and mayhem, has now been clearly seen for what it is in Syria. This provides US-UK Intelligence with an open door to influence those who are vulnerable, threatened, and have some hope of being saved from ISIS oppression if the West stays engaged militarily, particularly with the presence of US-UK special forces in non-Assad controlled enclaves. The latter are political–military decisions but should be underscored by sound intelligence that indicates where and how the most effective counter-ISIS propaganda and recruitment tools and funds can be employed. One area where UK–US Intelligence intervention can be most efficacious in the 2020s is in the countering of ISIS recruitment of professionals, such as scientist's administrators, engineers, technologists, and economists, to manage ISIS-controlled industry, agriculture, and trade wherever it appears and that is clearly under ISIS direct control. For example, ISIS was able with external financial support from the other Sunni-dominated states in the region, to operate the dam on the Assad Lake, a thermal power plant near Aleppo, petroleum enterprises, and claims by ISIS that it issues its own currency. Future ISIS-related critical infrastructure and logistics can be thwarted by UK–US intelligence operations in conjunction with political–military- diplomatic actions. Many ISIS specialists and consultants have come from Western countries. US-UK Intelligence and the Five Eyes as a whole have the means to identify such people, isolate them, and dissuade them from association with a terrorist organization, a serious crime in Western states, and certainly in the Five Eyes countries. UK–US intelligence will also have to divert energy to collection and analysis of internal ISIS perspectives and self-assessments, as ISIS continues to face internal problems. These are difficult to gauge unless serious programs are initiated to both assess and then disrupt ISIS internal theocratic propaganda and its core organization, especially funding, weapon supplies, and recruitment media. HUMINT has a serious role in this process and collaborative operations with non-Five Eyes collectors will be important. If internal dissent is created within ISIS, then it may lose most of its territorial ambitions under pressure from regional forces. Jordan, for example, joined the Kurds and independent elements in Syria and Iraq in their struggle. Sowing disagreements between ISIS's leaders is potentially as valuable as alienating them in drone strikes and other kinetic means. To date neither Saudi Arabia nor Qatar has been able to control ISIS leaders. The creation of rifts by the Five Eyes community together with pressure from both the West, the United Nations, and the Sunni Islamic states could aggregate to undermine the ISIS leadership, and ultimately lead to its capitulation. ISIS's main objective to conjoin the Sunni space will have been undermined if, in the 2020s, well-organized and coordinated Western opposition with regional allies contains ISIS's spread. ISIS's "future map" of the 2010s will look like a pipedream. If the right things are executed, it is very unlikely that ISIS will be able to have a major support base beyond Syria and Iraq. However, if the Five Eyes intelligence infrastructure does not maintain a major intelligence collection and assessment capability in this key region in support of national policies, then the future will remain ambiguous. If ISIS regenerates a foothold of any kind in Syria it is very unlikely to make inroads in the face of President Bashar al-Assad's forces, supported by the Russian Army, Special Forces, and Air Force, arms supply, and other covert Russian operations. The main aim of the Bashar al-Assad regime has been to exterminate local radical terrrorist groups and to stabilize the remaining territories, and then to recover the economy in the context of a lost Euphrates. All this remains to be seen. The Syrian scenario is further complicated by relations between Syria and Israel, and their primary supporters and military benefactors, Russia and the United States respectively. US-UK Intelligence, the Five Eyes, and their Western allies need to exploit relations between ISIS, Saudi Arabia and Qatar. ISIS atrocities and a clear divergence from fundamental Moslem teaching can polarize opposition to ISIS, leaving the Islamists isolated and surrounded, facing a demise akin to those 20th-century tyrannies that sought to impose their will by brutal suppression and atrocities. ISIS will have hopefully masterminded its own downfall, by brutally violating all the norms of human conduct and indeed the very essence of the prophet's words. Cruelty, inhumanity, and sheer violent atrocity have no place in the civilized world and the UK and US should play their key intelligence roles in ensuring that ISIS reaps the whirlwind of its own making. The Five Eyes together with political initiatives by the United States, the United Kingdom, Jordan, and their allies in the Middle East and Europe have a clear moral and "just war" mandate to destroy the backbone of ISIS that ha masterminded atrocities. At the end of World War II, the US pursued one of the most far-seeing strategies to turn around a country that had perpetrated the worst kind of atrocities and war crimes in history. This model, the reverse of the Versailles Treaty model, signed on June 28, 1919, was created by George Marshall and the American leadership. Once ISIS is defeated, indeed obliterated, the extraordinarily demanding challenge will be for the US and its allies to find just and equitable ways to resolve the complexities of the Sunni–Shi'a territorial and theocratic space. It will require immense humanity to steer through the vastly troubled waters of Sunni and Shi'a rivalries and centuries of theocratic divergence. This is at the very heart of the issues in the Middle East. The lost opportunity after the Iraq intervention-invasion to separate Sunni, Shi'a, and Kurd into defined geographic and theocratic political territories may have been lost, resulting in an ancient sectarian divide that then engaged in bloody conflict, but all things are possible in the Middle East, and US-UK Intelligence will have a critical role in supplying highly reliable intelligence to frame what will have to be new and innovative diplomatic initiatives. The Israel–Palestinian Challenge:

The events of October 7, 2023 have resounded around the world. They have polarized decades long issues relating to the "Two State" solution between Israel and the Palestinians, represented by the Palestinian Authority. The crisis brought to the forefront the critical need to find a long term solution and the maintenance of peace not just between Israel and Palestinians, also the wider Arab world and the major democracies. The history leading up to October 7th, 2023 is complex. During his presidency (2009–2017), Barack Obama proclaimed that he wished to see Israel return to the pre-1967 June War boundaries in accordance with United Nations Security Council Resolution 242, passed at the end of the 1967 June War. President Obama argued that this was a critical prerequisite to begin a truly long-term solution to the Israel–Palestinian situation. His administration's position rested on the fundamental UN concept embodied in Resolution 242 that Israel took land that was not Israel's by force and that in order to meet Palestinian rights to nationhood and wider Arab demands, that the Golan Heights and the West Bank be restored to their lawful owners. These were strident demands and were in keeping with United Nation's resolutions. It should be noted that according to the Department of Peace and Conflict Research in Uppsala, Sweden, Israel has been sanctioned in 45 resolutions by the UN Human Rights Council for various violations regarding the Palestinian situation. Much earlier, between 1967 (shortly after the end of the 1967 June War) and 1989 the UN Security Council adopted 131 resolutions directly addressing the Arab–Israeli conflict. What this demonstrates is the need for constant accurate

UK–US intelligence across all domains affecting the ongoing Israel–Palestinian situation. This is complicated by the United States unique relationship with Israel, making an already complex situation for the other four nations of the Five Eyes intelligence agencies even more sensitive. The United Nations General Assembly has adopted a number of resolutions stating that the United States' relationship with Israel encourages Israeli expansionist policies, particularly in the West Bank. This complicates life for the UK, Canadian, Australian, and New Zealand intelligence agencies and the political systems that they support individually and collectively. For example, the 9th Emergency Session of the UN General Assembly was convened at the request of the UN Security Council because the United States refused to adopt sanctions against Israel. The US has tended to follow what became called the "Negroponte Doctrine" (after John Negroponte, US Ambassador to the United Nations, September 2001–June 2004) that opposes any Security Council resolutions that criticize or sanction Israel without also denouncing militant Palestinian activities by Hamas and Hezbollah. Collecting and analyzing impartial intelligence in this environment becomes demanding not so much because of the sources and methods involved but because of relationships within the Five Eyes that are driven by the national foreign policies of each of the individual countries. For example, at the same time that the Five Eyes are tracking illicit arms transfers from Iran to Hamas and Hezbollah, they also have to keep close watch on Israeli covert operations in the United States and the other Five Eyes countries for conducting both classical espionage and also intellectual property penetration and collection, particularly of sensitive military technology or other commercial technology that Israel deems desirable for sustaining and expanding its economy. There are inherent conflicts in this complex scenario, particularly in even more conflicting scenarios where for instance Israeli military intelligence and clandestine service (the Mossad) may from time to time provide timely and valuable intelligence. For example, the latter may include Iranian sanction violations, covert arms shipments, and Russian–Syrian operations. The overall situation since the 1967 June War has been exacerbated more recently by more proactive US policies in favor of Israel and the Trump administration's withdrawal of substantial aid to the Palestinians. The move of the US Embassy from Tel Aviv to Jerusalem also caused friction within the Five Eyes political–diplomatic community. The Trump administration's announcement on March 25, 2019 to support Israel's claims to permanent sovereignty and possession of the Golan Heights drew global anger. The fall-out remains to be seen. Syria's ally, Russia, will likely not stand by and do nothing, with an extant UN resolution in their favor that may give both countries legitimacy in a range of possible options. Obama had already used this resolution as a basis for Israel returning territory occupied since the 1967 June War. This situation is a potential tinderbox waiting to be ignited by perhaps reckless adventurism by all the key protagonists. However, US-UK Intelligence has to remain aloof in the future from such differences and produce unvarnished and impartial intelligence reports. President Netanyahu of Israel reacted vehemently to several Obama White House statements, stressing to multiple international audiences that in any two-state solution to the Israeli–Palestinian situation, Israel must have what he defines as "defensible boundaries." He saw a return to the 1967 status quo as giving up territory that is vital for Israel's survival in the event of various military and economic scenarios. His opposite number, President Abbas, and several US Secretaries of State have fully understood the reasons for his declarations. However, many independent international relations specialists on Middle East affairs have stated that if the peace process is ever to enter a substantively new era from the prior decades, and if the Palestinians are indeed ever to accede, as Israel did, to become a nation state within the community of nations, clearly more has to happen than declarations, whether rhetorical or otherwise.

The UN Resolution 242:

There has been considerable analysis over the years since 1967 of the intent of the wording of Resolution 242, drafted by the then British Ambassador to the United Nations, Lord Caradon. The resolution is to most lawyers and international specialists quite explicit, precise and well worded with no ambiguity. However, the wording that has caused most analysis is the section of the resolution that says, in affirmation of Article 2 of the UN Charter, the United Nations Security Council affirms: "Termination of all claims or states of belligerency and respect for and acknowledgment of the sovereignty, territorial integrity and political independence of every state in the area and their right to live in peace within secure and recognized boundaries free from threats or acts of force." Within this section the words that cause most disagreement are, "rights to live in peace within secure and recognized boundaries." The Israelis and President Netanyahu have been explicit in stating that any redrawing of the pre-1967 June War boundaries, now essentially the West Bank of the Jordan River and the Golan Heights, since Israel has withdrawn from the Sinai, must be so that Israel can be secure. The latter has been defined by President Netanyahu as being "defensible boundaries." To most military and US-UK Intelligence personnel this phrase has significant and very definable connotations. In looking back briefly to the 1960s, the Middle East was a critical part of the Cold War stand off and a hot bed for playing out the international rivalries between the United States and the Soviet Union. Israel felt naturally threatened and surrounded by potential belligerents that were encouraged and supported by Moscow. By June of 1967 the situation reached boiling point. The sudden preemptive strikes made by Israel to seize territory from Egypt, Syria, and Jordan to extend its boundaries and create defensive barriers were extremely successful. Israel's actions precipitated a crisis that all but plunged the United States into a conflict with the Soviet Union. This could have occurred if Israel advanced beyond the Golan Heights towards Damascus, followed by Soviet intervention. Very well-documented research has shown how the Soviet Union would have launched forces against Israel if they had continued in their march towards Damascus from the Golan Heights. The world has changed with the demise of the Soviet Union, and in its aftermath have emerged equally compelling threats to Middle East stability, not least the rise of Iran and the emergence of several parties and groups that espouse terrorism as a vehicle for achieving political goals. Other state and non-state players have become either directly or indirectly involved through the supply of arms, training, and other equipment. It is very easy to forget that terrorism is not a recent phenomenon. It has been vehicle for change in the Middle East since World War II. President Menachem Begin of Israel was a member of Irgun, an organization dubbed by the international community as a violent and extremist terrorist organization and described by David Ben-Gurion, national founder and first Prime Minister of the state of Israel, as the "enemy of the Jewish people." Begin saw himself as a freedom fighter, not a terrorist. It is easy to forget that in the Middle East the past is often prologue. Hamas and Hezbollah pursue political goals often by unacceptable violent means, most often dubbed terrorist acts by the international community. Such factions cite the same principles in working for the creation of an independent Palestinian state that the post-war Israeli "terrorists" cited to justify their violent actions in seeking the creation of the independent state of Israel. It is very easy to lose this perspective, while at the same time condemning, as the international community should indeed do, any acts of terrorism, whatever the goal. In 1977, Menachem Begin, the man born a Russian Jew and persecuted by both the Nazis and the Soviets, became Prime Minister of Israel. Begin was responsible for the peace treaty with Anwar Sadat of Egypt that returned the Sinai to Egypt, and which led to both men winning the Nobel Peace Prize. What this demonstrates is that all things are possible, even though in 1946 Begin had led the bombing of the King David Hotel in Jerusalem, and in March 1952 the attempt on the life of Chancellor Konrad Adenauer of West Germany. UK–US Intelligence has to operate within this hugely complex historic backdrop, providing intelligence that will help both maintain Middle East stability and providing the warnings and indicators that certain events may precipitate potentially catastrophic consequences that may impact the global peace and economy. Intelligence and Politics: The Clear Need for Separation: Today the Sunni Islamist group Hamas that has run the Gaza portion of the Palestinian Territories, and Hezbollah, the Shi'a Muslim militant group and political party in Lebanon, appear very much like how Irgun looked in 1942 when it split from the Haganah, launching from 1944–1948 a campaign against the British in Palestine. On May 14, 1948 the State of Israel was created. The relevance and poignancy are clear: Israel was fundamentally born out of terrorism. The key for UK–US Intelligence is to have collection systems in place today that will help in providing accurate information to guide international policies to prevent the spread of terrorism, while clearly finding a solution to the above policy dilemmas. Some analysts see the answer perhaps lying with Jordan and Israel, supported by the United States and its key allies. However, the ever more volatile situation in Syria, aided and abetted by Russia, adds another regional complexity, plus the ongoing crisis in the Yemen, and a range of Saudi-led activities and operations that have caused not just discord within the United Nations, but also within the Five Eyes foreign policy elites, both inside and outside their current governments. US-UK Intelligence community has to remain aloof from controversy in order to perform effectively. Moreover, the US and UK have to choose their intelligence allies not just wisely, but with continuous circumspection based on the detailed exigencies of a particular scenario.

The 2018 book, *Rise and Kill: The Secret History of Israel's Targeted Assassinations*, (Random House, New York) by Ronen Bergman shows how decades of covert Israeli assassination operations, mainly by the Mossad, pre- and post-independence in 1948, may appear to have temporary short-term gains but in the long term fail to address the ultimate key strategic considerations, particularly a solution to the Israel–Palestinian territorial dilemma. This is the root cause perhaps of all Israel's problems that galvanize the international community, other than perhaps the United States, against its policies and operations, while the advanced democracies equally condemn the continuous bloodshed by both sides' clandestine and terrorist forces. President Netanyahu's strategic concerns for the "defensive boundaries" of Israel are clearly demarcated by geography, the distance between key locations in Israel and the West Bank are on the order of six to nine miles, with a huge concentration of the Israeli population on the coastal strip where most of Israel's commercial and industrial life resides. His perfectly reasonable concern is that the West Bank provides a buffer area and site for defensive missile systems that will ward off an attack. The key to helping President Netanyahu and the Israeli people find both peace and security some argue may lie with Jordan. Jordan is perhaps the most stable political regime in the Arab world. King Abdullah leads a nation that is making significant progress in both democratization and improvement in the lives of the ordinary Jordanian, while providing bedrock security against outside extremist influences. Israel has to both respect and trust Jordan, and Jordan's security against outside threats has to be underpinned by equal aid from the United States, just as the United States provides aid to Israel. The likelihood of a destabilizing and anti-Israel regime emerging in Jordan is at present very remote. UK–US intelligence in the 2020s will have to monitor carefully Jordanian stability. The threats to Israel lie much further to the east in Iran, and that country's extremist associations with other state and non-state actors. By the same token Jordan is equally threatened by extremist groups from outside that will try to destabilize an otherwise progressive regime, with the vast majority of Jordanians loyal both to their political processes and their head of state. Modern cruise and ballistic missile technology are such that the West Bank buffer zone is not relevant for Israel in terms of a ground-attack invasion from the east, particularly given relationships with both Jordan and the underpinnings provided by the United States. The major threats to both countries, other than extremist attacks from terrorist groups, are most likely to come from missile attacks. The very worst scenario for Israel would be a preemptive ballistic missile attack from Iran. In this and other missile scenarios the West Bank does not play as a key geographic entity because of speed, times, and distance issues associated with the location of key targets in both Jordan and Israel if attacked by cruise and ballistic missiles. Some strategists argue that the West Bank can play a role insofar as it could be the site for a layered defensive missile network. What the above illustrates is the critical intelligence underpinnings for both warnings and indicators but also for supporting policy decisions and military planning. Some argue that a settlement with Jordan over the West Bank can includethe following: Jordan regains control of the West Bank and with United States oversight begins the management of both Palestinian and Israeli settlements in the area. In return, Jordan should grant to Israel several key sovereign air base sites in the West Bank where Israel may have full rights, permanent access for its military to man 24/7 defensive missile batteries and provide early warning radar systems. Such sites and systems will be of equal value to Jordan. In addition, it is argued that the United States could provide other key layers of defensive systems for both Jordan and Israel, in addition to the military systems that it provides under the various aid agreements. If these sorts of solution options are both realistic, achievable, and some form of progress is made in the 2020s, then UK–US intelligence will be critical for establishing highly reliable intelligence systems to ensure that risks are mitigated. From President Netanyahu's perspective the issue of the strategic role of the West Bank has now taken on a whole new complexion, and one that guarantees Israeli access and presence for the above defensive systems. This is all hypothesis but whatever does occur in the Middle East in the next ten-plus years will require a significant intelligence input that is not driven solely by US interests. The United States will also want to minimize deployment costs, except at times of rising tension in the region. The independence and capabilities of the other four nations of the Five Eyes intelligence community will be hugely significant in terms of independent and unvarnished assessments. Intelligence sharing is critical in any negotiation and agreement and both Jordan and Israel will need to build confidence with themselves and mutually with the United States in order to share time-sensitive intelligence, complicated by the roles of Russia and China intervening at all levels of political– diplomatic–military–economic–arms sales activities. Put simply, good intelligence is about providing information to the user that enables them to make well-informed decisions well ahead of a decision point, never to be surprised, and always to have the upper-hand knowledge base over one's actual or potential adversary. The Hamas attack on Israel and the subsequent major counter attack by Israel on Gaza has caused approbation in many parts of the democratic countries of the world, with for example Australia, Canada, and New Zealand voting with the majority in the United Nations, against the United States' position, for a cease fire in Gaza when the death toll of innocent men, women and children reached appalling numbers. Many in the international community condemned Israel's attacks on civilian positions in Gaza as war crimes and crimes against humanity, no different in other words than the original October 7, 2023 attack by Hamas on innocent Israeli civilians, an equally appalling war crime and crime against humanity. To maintain future peace the more positive Arab nations not aligned with Iran and Syria will have to lead equally with the United States and other positive well meaning countries within the United Nations in finding a lasting solution between Israel and the Palestinians. Gaza will also have to be rebuilt after Israel's onslaught on homes, businesses, hospitals, schools, and infrastructure.

The Global Challenge from China:

The emerging global power of China and its challenge to US military strength in East Asia poses fundamental questions about the nature and goals of Chinese policy for the long term, and how US-UK Intelligence can provide intelligence to help craft a strategy both in their best interests and in those of its friends and allies, not just in the region but worldwide. In July 2019 the Chinese government published "China's National Defense in the New Era". This articulates China's public version of its defense policy. It is explicit about Taiwan and its "One China principle" and that if necessary, it will fight for Taiwan. These are words to heed. China's stated GDP expenditures on defense and as a percentage of Chinese government spending are revealing, if accurate, and when compared with the GDP defense expenditures thatthe Chinese quote between 2012–2017 of the US (3.5%), Russia (4.4%), India (2.5%), the UK (2%), France (2.3%), Japan (1%), and Germany (1.2%). China states it spends 1.3% of GDP on defense. There is one statement that also resonates: "China firmly believes that hegemony and expansion are doomed to failure." We assume that China means territorial expansion by aggressive means. This is at odds with China's militarization of the Spratly Islands. So, the question is, "Quo Vadis China?" The rise of China is self-evident, but the huge question exists as to what are China's long-and short-term goals, whose economic drivers, let alone military expansion, are reshaping the international security land and seascapes? At the same time the United States rejected under President Trump the multilateral economic and political framework, witnessed by withdrawal from the Trans-Pacific Partnership, renegotiation of NAFTA, and threats to leave the World Trade Organization, compounded by punitive tariffs on China and US allies, and rejection of the Iran Nuclear Agreement signed by key European allies, Russia, and China. The effect of all this was been to draw nations into the Chinese orbit, create disharmony with US NATO allies, and draw Russia and China closer. Punitive US sanctions have led to hugely negative consequences. The Biden Administration has at the time or writing in 2024 sought to reverse all the negative effects of the Trump Administration. These have been largely successful, particularly in reenergizing NATO-US relations. This success was emblematic when Russia invaded Ukraine in February, 2022. Most of all is the extraordinary successful growth of China's "Belt and Road Initiative" (BRI), a 21st-century "Silk Road" started in 2013, a trillion dollar investment that embraces about 80 countries, strategically designed to guarantee that China will not only secure its own energy, trade routes, and key natural resources, but also expand its investment in global port infrastructure and sea routes across all the world's oceans, stimulating demand for Chinese products and acquiring economic control through massive investments and loans that will not be repaid in some cases this century. China has also articulated a "Polar Silk Road," stating that it is a "Near Arctic State." The means to achieve what are clearly stated Chinese goals is a "Maritime Grand Strategy," with the Chinese Navy the key centerpiece. China seeks to gain access to and control of precious metal extraction and production in Russia, Central Asia, Latin America, and Africa. China's "Debt Diplomacy" is reaping benefits at the expense of the United States and its key allies. It enables China to soften hitherto strained relations with Japan, the Philippines, and Vietnam, lessening the friction resulting from Chinese occupation and militarization of the Spratly and Paracel islands in the South China Sea. The latter is overtly geared to creating a presence to counter the US Seventh Fleet, while enabling China 200 nautical-mile territorial claims to fishing and undersea resource rights around each and every atoll and island, in spite of the International Court of Arbitration's declaration that China has no such legal or historic claims. The US has not attempted to enforce the ruling of the court in The Hague. Meanwhile China has built naval facilities across the Indian Ocean in Gwadar, Pakistan, in Hambantota in Sri Lanka, and Djibouti, with long-term port agreements with Cambodia, Indonesia, Malaysia, Brunei, Myanmar, Bangladesh, Tanzania, Namibia, Greece, and Italy. In the context of all the above the key question arises in 2024, how best to maintain peace and avoid war with China, particularly with the Taiwan issue overhanging all aspects of political-military-economic-diplomatic dealings between the United States and its allies and China. Two successive US National Security Advisors, Tom Donilon, a Washington lawyer, (2010–2013) and Susan Rice, a policy aficionado (2013–2017), let all this happen with zero US counter actions with the hawkish John Bolton, more preoccupied with provoking conflict with Iran rather than paying attention to the detail that James Fanell provided in his briefing of the House Permanent Select Committee on Intelligence in May 2018. A trade and resource conflict is inevitable unless the United States shifts gears to a political–diplomatic–economic turn-around strategy, underwritten by the power of the United States Navy and Marine Corps, the forward-deployed round-the-clock presence that guarantees freedom of the seas a rule-based international order, and the prevention of conflict over trade, resources, and those critical minerals deemed vital for not just national security but the very heart and soul of the continuing digital revolution and its massive product line. China is following the British maritime strategy and economic model that it pursued for centuries—the defense of seaborne trade and its support of overseas acquisitions and influence. China is investing "Without Risk," with zero shareholders to please. Investment in African mines brings nothing like the risk to US anf European investors. China is stealing technology not just through well-known cyber penetration and espionage but a simple and successful economic strategy—US and other foreign investors have and are going to China, investing, and then finding that China replicates their technology, production, and engineering plans, and then creates home-grown industries and companies. Foreign investment has and will die on the vine in due course. The response from the United States and its key NATO allies has been appallingly paltry. Former Secretary of Defense, Jim Mattis, a wise and wonderfully astute US Marine General, has rightly observed that one key counterbalance is the "strategic convergence" of India and the United States, together with other key US allies, because otherwise Chinese hegemony in the Indo-Pacific region at the economic, political, and strategic levels, will predominate. The huge danger of this is a 21st-century version and tragic specter of the 1930s economic implosion in East Asia that set Japan on not just a conflict course at sea but territorial aggrandizement that led to catastrophe for the world and dénouement on December 7, 1941. The global economy, the world, simply cannot afford to witness another conflict on this scale. There will be no winners, only losers all round. The United States and its allies, including convergence with India, must face this challenge with unprecedented diplomatic, economic, and political–military skill and fortitude. Some of James Fanell's testimony was challenged by other experts, particularly his prognosis that China may invade Taiwan at some point in the 2020s. Notwithstanding this aspect, his detailed description of China's expansionist policies and actions were thoroughly grounded in accurate intelligence. Moreover, he made the salient point that much of what China has done in the past 10 years before his testimony was clearly stated in their open literature. In other words, the Chinese have not attempted to hide their plans and programs. They have told us in no uncertain terms what they plan to do. It is possible for the United States in particular to slip into a position of action and reaction vis-à-vis increased Chinese military capabilities and operations seemingly intent on challenging the United States. China is overtly demonstrating what Chinese official writings convey, namely that the American East Asian presence will be challenged and that China sees itself as the preeminent Asian power, with an intent to create a hegemony that will in due course extend to the outer island chains of the Western Pacific. Action and reaction were very much phenomena of the Cold War: The Soviet Union would develop a capability, or extend its influence in various areas, or establish a new base, and the United States and NATO would counter such activities. The great game played itself out until the demise of the Soviet Union. What the United States and its allies must seriously consider now are the potentially negative impacts of following a similar pattern of behavior with China, of being led astray into costly and complex situations at all levels of political–military strategy. There are alternative ways to address the issues, problems, and challenges that lie ahead for the new generation of American leaders, who cannot afford the luxury of a Cold War standoff with massive economic implications. However, what the above does show quite clearly is that UK–US Intelligence and their Five Eyes partners, together with Japan, India, and other East Asia allies will need to be extremely vigilant in the warnings and indicators domain, such that their political leaderships cannot be caught unawares by sudden and perhaps unprecedented drastic actions by China. It is wise initially to revert to first principles when beginning the analysis that will lead to creating an enduring strategy for the US and its allies in East Asia. DoesChina resemble, or has it begun to replicate, the patterns of activities that have characterized the growth, and decline, of imperial powers and those nations that's ought regional hegemony? Do the imperial models of ancient Greece and Rome, the Spanish, British, Hapsburg, Turkish, and Russian empires resemble and apply to what we see evolving in China? Do the militarist, expansionist territorial goals of Napoleon, the Nazis, Fascist Italy, and Imperial Japan connect with what we observe is happening with a growing Chinese military capability, an economic juggernaut that is by no means yet in top gear, and with massive resource needs, particularly oil, that require overseas Chinese investment, foreign port facilities, and overseas political–military infrastructure? The answer to much of the above is that China has led an extremely non-invasive approach to international relations in modern times, with certain exceptions. The past 500 years, since the European powers began their outward growth, exploration, colonization, and empire building, have witnessed China on a very different track. In that time, China has never invaded and permanently occupied a sovereign state or shown imperial intent. Since the Chinese revolution and the conclusion of World War II, China has for the most part lived inwardly. But there have been exceptions. General Douglas MacArthur's 1950 foray northwards into North Korea and to the Yalu River provoked a response from China that was not surprising: Its forces invaded south across the Yalu River and drove the United States back to the 39th parallel. From the Chinese perspective, the United States posed a threat to Chinese sovereignty and to a communist client state. In 1962, during the short Sino-Indian War, China invaded India briefly as a means of letting Jawaharlal Nehru's government know that China disapproved of India's support for the Dalai Lama and the Tibetan independence movement. After India suffered a defeat, China quickly withdrew having made its point However, the Chinese invasion of Vietnam in February 1979, to signal Chinese disapproval of Vietnam's invasion of Cambodia to suppress China's client regime, the Khmer Rouge, led to an ignominious defeat. The war lasted just one month. China lost about 20,000 troops, more in a matter of weeks than the United States lost in a single year of fighting in Vietnam. Moreover, a Vietnamese force of 100,000 border troops bloodied a Chinese army of 250,000, a humiliating defeat. The impact on China's leader, Deng Xiaoping, was dramatic.

China has supplied weapons and technology to nation-states that run counter to US and its allies' interests. China has distinctive and clear-cut policies regarding all major international issues, whether it is UN policy in the Middle East or policy toward rogue nations (of which North Korea is a leading example). China, like any other country, pursues what it believes to be its national self-interest. US-UK Intelligence will have to monitor carefully Chinese pronouncements and actions so that changes do not come as surprises. What China has *not* done is provide indications that it sees territorial expansion by invasion of other nations territories as a way to extend Chinese power and influence. It has mostly followed international law and agreements. There is no question that China could have marched into Hong Kong or Macau at any time without resistance. Instead, China waited until the legal expiration of treaty agreements that, in 21st-century hindsight, amounted to the blunt use of 19th-century imperial power by Portugal and Britain. Both territories were transitioned peacefully to Chinese rule. By contrast, an Argentinean dictatorship decided in 1982 to challenge Britain's long-standing rights and ownership of the Falkland Islands, and suffered the consequences. China has never made such moves. If there is a deviation from this trend, it may be economic and not militarist, and could in due course prove to be the seed of serious discord, the resource-hungry dragon. However, there are intelligence signs that the above may be too rosy a prognosis, that the Grand Maritime Strategy which China is clearly pursuing is a potential precursor to denouement. US-UK Intelligence will be pivotal in this regard. China has repeatedly indicated that its inherent needs and destiny are bound to economic hegemony in East Asia. To that end, the People's Republic has begun a systematic set of claims, based on perceived historic rights, to key uninhabited reefs, atolls, and small islands in the South China Sea. China is now a self-evident economic Goliath. At some point its gross national product will equal and likely surpass those of the United States, Japan, and Germany. The danger is not economic competition, which is healthy and beneficial in the context of a well-managed, globally interconnected marketplace, but resource needs. China's massive population requires to be fed and sustained in keeping with its world economic position. China has a serious hold on key precious metals, particularly in the semiconductor and space industries, but in other areas it is woefully dependent. Oil is the largest problem. The exponential growth of Chinese oil demand could reach a possible supply and demand crisis situation in the mid to late 2020s. The country's planners are constantly looking for alternative suppliers and areas for investment and exploration. China is still using coal as a major energy source. The Western powers with green energy and, conservation issues high on their national agendas see the Paris Accord as critical for all nations, and especially the two huge-population states of China and India, requiring increasing large investments in green solar, wind, and hydro energy sources. There is no question that potentially both these nations can convert with the right leadership and investment to alternative energy sources. UK–US intelligence will have to increasingly invest in economic intelligence, coupling their sources and methods with highly capable analyses from industry and especially the more prestigious academic institutions tracking global energy sources and distribution. The specter of a resource-hungry China replicating the Japanese resource-driven expansion policies of the 1930s which culminated in the attack on Pearl Harbor, is not in sight in any shape of form at present or the foreseeable future. The US and the UK will have to increasingly devote more resources to economic intelligence in the strategic sense. Chinese seizure of small islands and atolls in the South China Sea, and the militarization of these with runways, missile sites, radar and communications, exacerbated by aggressive naval posturing underpinning what the international legal community has declared as illegal claims to the Spratly and Paracel islands, are clearly matters of very serious concern. The Five Eyes have collected extensive intelligence on all these developments and the public domain commercial satellite imagery of the Chinese South China Sea sites has made it evident to the world community what the Chinese have done in construction terms, showing in global media source their clear intent. This is in flagrant violation of the of the International Court of Arbitration in The Hague, finding against Chinese claims in the South China Sea as not based on any legitimate historic rights or antecedents. To US-UK Intelligence and the Five Eyes community these actions reflect a likely Chinese policy to continue militarization and claims not founded in the United Nations Convention on the Law of the Sea. All this indicates willful intent to ignore international law, a most worrisome posture. The US Navy and its allies are currently challenging all Chinese claims in the South China Sea by exercising regularly the rights of innocent passage within the historic international limits in all the areas claimed to be Chinese territory, by sailing aircraft carriers, cruisers and destroyers into those waters that the Chinese claim as sovereign. This has led to near collisions at sea of Chinese and US warships and other hostile Chinese acts, such as intercepting US aircraft in international airspace that the Chinese claim as their national airspace. None of this bodes well for the future as the Chinese expand their navy in both numbers and capabilities, far exceeding what may be regarded as the classic naval mission of the protection of seaborne trade. The legal concept of a 200-mile economic zone has been generally accepted into the body of international law, but that zone and the law of the sea are the least developed and codified legalisms within the international community. Drawing 200-mile economic zones around the disputed island chains of the South China Sea creates major challenges for dispute resolution. Vietnam has been at odds with China over island sovereignty issues for some time, and the geopolitics of the region place Japan, the Philippines, South Korea, Malaysia, Thailand, Singapore, and

Indonesia in potential conflict with China over such claims as well. The wider issue of Chinese resource needs will not fade away. There are no signs of major green energy programs that will solve China's problems any time soon. Coupled to China's increasing thirst for oil is its parallel policy of hard-currency accumulation and owning foreign indebtedness. What then, may China really want to achieve, given its military buildup, its naval exercises, and its posturing regarding Taiwan? What does China hope to gain by its ability to field new weapons systems that US-UK Intelligence and the Five Eyes have assiduously monitored and analyzed? The latter include anti-carrier, anti-access ballistic missiles, and anti-satellite systems, together with a considerable investment in electronic and cyber warfare skills and technology, and a growing fleet of submarines, both nuclear and non-nuclear, along with increasing moves into space and other intelligence/surveillance/reconnaissance domains. China has hypersonic missile systems and the latest intelligence has revealed capable long range high speed drones. The Five Eyes community is concerned that China may, very simply, be planning on winning a war that it never fights. What is the essence of this analysis? Such a war is about countervailing power, raising the order of battle of key assets to high levels, and creating constant challenges that require persistent US and allied presence, deployments, and basing at very high cost. At one level it may be regarded as a war of attrition by other means, underpinned by sustainable economic growth and a Chinese military–industrial complex based on the new Chinese State capitalist model, which even some distinguished American economists have cited as being more efficient than the free-market capitalist model. US-UK Intelligence analysts then have to ask, is this is a new form of hegemony, or a unique Chinese version? The threat is not just the military buildup per se, but the underlying single weakness in the otherwise rosy Chinese future: resource limitations and the increasing demand for oil, and what is already being witnessed in Africa, with massive Chinese investment that is clearly resource oriented, particularly minerals. By beefing up its military strength, China wins the war it never fights by checkmating the United States, specifically the US Seventh Fleet, the key forward-deployed Asian representative of American presence, intent, technology, and firepower. The intelligence to date does not bode well. China is pursuing quite simply a massive military modernization, with naval operations across the whole Indo-Pacific region, and put very directly, predatory economics. China is constantly strengthening the "Maritime Silk Road" in the Indian Ocean and demonstrating preparations for both combat and non-combat operations in the Indian Ocean, a huge change frompre-2010. In January 2016 China signed a ten-year agreement with Djibouti for port access and basing rights, ostensibly to protect Chinese commercial interests and citizens in Africa, and support counter-terrorist operations. At the same time this base provides China with a strategic posture adjacent to the critical Bab-el-Mandab Strait. Similarly, with Chinese basing rights at the deep-water port of Gwadar, Pakistan, at Salalah in Oman, and in the Seychelles. In May 2019 China indicated that it would invest $10.7 billion in Oman. China will undoubtedly create "listening stations" inall these locations, as well as becoming a major arms supplier to the former US ally, Pakistan. All the ports in which China is investing are or will become "dual use" ports for commercial shipping and Chinese Navy port visits, repair and maintenance, and as key logistics hubs distant from mainland China. By the early 2020s China had the world's largest navy, signaling that China is no longer a land power but a maritime power whose trade is currently about 41% of GDP, and of that trade about 95% is seaborne. In 2020 China had about 5,000 known registered ships. So, what is the best strategy for the United States and its allies, and what requirements will be placed on Us-UK Intelligence? First, none of the Five Eyes nations can contemplate a war with China. However, no responsible US leader can abide China creating an East Asian economic–political–military hegemony that may witness the demise of US influence, and with it, critical American economic interests. The Five Eyes navies led by the United States Navy plus other key regional allies such as Japan, India, and South Korea will have to return to a more regular and expansive presence in Far Eastern waters. This is critical to keeping the economic arteries healthy by the wise use of naval power. US-UK Intelligence and the Five Eyes become the centerpiece of the intelligence gathering and analysis to support these operations.

The solution may perhaps lie within the problem itself. While the United States reacts to Chinese moves—planning, for example, ways to implement new air-sea anti–access tactics and capabilities— essential points are possibly being missed. China's quest for economic hegemony by political–military means, in essence its Grand Maritime Strategy, can be addressed at the strategic level, because the United States and its allies have several critical factors in their favor. In the strategy that evolves from these factors, the US Navy, the other Five Eyes navies and major Asian allies, are important players. All will require coherent, accurate, and timely intelligence. East and Southeast Asia and the wider Indo-Pacific region, stretching from the Malacca Straits across the Indian Ocean to east Africa and the key entry points to the Persian Gulf and the Red Sea, are joined economically, and therefore politically, by one medium—the sea. It is the means by which most of the trade of Asia, and thus the world, takes place. Seaborne commerce is the enduring thread that runs through the history of the world since the age of discovery and expansion. Without oceanic trade, the global economy would collapse. The sea routes connecting all the Asian countries with the rest of the world are vital arteries. If, for whatever reason, they cease to function, the world will hemorrhage economically. The disparate Asian nations are interconnected and interdependent in this regard. The vital passages of the Malacca Straits and the Indonesian Archipelago run the routes that take trade onward through the South China Sea, the East China Sea, the Yellow Sea, the Sea of Japan, the Pacific Islands, and the trans-Pacific routes; those aquatic pathways are the lifelines of the world's trading nations. The protection of that trade, the maintenance of the freedom of the seas, and the enforcement of the laws of the sea present a huge strategic opportunity to bring together the Five Eyes nations and their allies in the region. Such a common effort can foster long-term peace and prosperity for all, and ensure that East Asia is not destabilized by misplaced Chinese hegemonic intentions, underwritten by a clearly articulated Grand Maritime Strategy. China does not win a war that it never fights, and Asia can grow in wealth and prosperity with its Five Eyes and other key trading partners. This can be the genesis of a new strategy in Asia, one based on trade-route protection, maritime power, shared efforts based on shared interests, and supported in all regards by high-quality Five Eyes intelligence sources, methods, and analysis. This strategy's key ingredients include freedom of navigation, freedom of the seas, protection of seaborne trade, and rights of passage. What is required is a new "Asian Law of the Sea," either written or declaratory. Such a law would:

- Guarantee various maritime rights, including defining territorial rights, rights of access and passage, fishing and resource rights, and codify maritime conduct.
- Provide unified policing and enforcement.
- Provide agreement-based (and, in due course, treaty-based) means for regular international gatherings of the member states.
- Take the Association of Southeast Asian Nations and other multi- and bilateral agreements to a new organization and forum for organizing and implementing a maritime code of conduct.

This new organization would be the vehicle for resolving issues associated with 200-mile economic zones and disputes over island chains; for enforcing international law and human rights; and for combating piracy, smuggling, and terrorism. That is a formidable array of international activities that the Five Eyes nations can carry out with their regional partners. Such a cooperative undertaking can be the means to bring China into the family of Asian nations in ways that are neither belligerent nor challenging to the status quo. The strategy clearly places markers in the sand. To be a non-participant is to take one's country out of the community of nations. If China chooses a less cooperative, continual hegemonic course, then its Asian neighbors will have built themselves a fortified maritime community, linked by various agreements and obligations that will be formidable. In this environment intelligence becomes absolutely vital. The most recent development of China creating bases and airfields from uninhabited reefs in disputed island areas in the South China Sea is a case in point. Open-source satellite imagery shows a clear Chinese intent to militarize these areas The alliance aspects are crucial. The good news is that the region's nations are on board. The Australians, the Malaysians, the Indonesians, the Thais, the South Koreans, the Japanese, the Philippines, and now the Vietnamese, signaled originally by US Secretary of Defense Robert Gates' successful groundbreaking visit back in late 2010, are increasingly joined in a common bond. At the center, in discreet fashion, has to be US-UK Intelligence and the Five Eyes as a whole, plus Japan and India, as the guardians against change, and worst case, surprise. The Five Eyes Navies and their close Asian allies are unique for multiple reasons, and one of them is the unifying force of the brotherhood of the sea that navies show toward one another. Sailors are gregarious people who are diplomats in myriad ways and nothing is more unifying than port visits after joint exercises, rescue missions, disaster relief, and successful operations against drug runners and terrorists. Navies by themselves can implement policies that no amount of conventional diplomacy can hope to achieve. The United States in particular has existing resources that require little additional investment to make security-force assistance with all the participating nations a permanent and persistent feature of US naval diplomacy. Those should be the watchwords of this strategy: "US naval diplomacy," supported by Five Eyes intelligence and complemented by the intelligence services of key regional allies, particularly Japan, India, and South Korea. Vietnam may increasingly become an intelligence player in the above mix. Joint international protection of maritime trade, economic rights, and the enforcement of a new emerging law of the sea for Asia can be the means to peaceful ends. If China balks and insists on an open standoff characterized by "benign aggression," then there is little that the United States and its friends and allies can do, other than to make it very clear that they will never tolerate any form of overt aggression. The olive branch can be continuously offered, and hopefully at some stage will be accepted with magnanimity. No one can successfully predict regime change in China. At present this seems highly unlikely. What one can perhaps hypothesize is that the confluence of generational change, the very international trade that is making China great, cultural and travel exchanges, the internet, and technological sharing will overcome the inwardness and control mechanisms of the Chinese leadership. The specter of Tiananmen Square still looms large. China demonstrates a ruthless streak from time to time, and the concern for human rights are not part of China's political make-up. Only time will tell if this will evolve. The virtues of youth and the global economy combined eventually may make certain political transformations inevitable in China. However, this may be a rose-tinted view given that China today monitors every citizen's personal telephones, the internet, and restricts communications in keeping with a 1930s-style dictatorship, while suppressing any form of dissent or opposition to policies such as the treatment of ethnic and religious minorities. One scenario can illustrate implementation of the new regional collective effort. Regular joint exercises, guided by excellent current intelligence and projections, can be executed to protect shipping following the routes from the Southeast Asian straits to the Japanese Islands and South Korea. Such exercises can develop and train the region's nations in all domains of maritime warfare and seaborne trade protection. For instance, in the antisubmarine-warfare and anti-surface modes, those nations can show both capability and will, and if China elects to be a thorn in the side of its neighbors by offering up a belligerent passive-aggressiveness, then it will merely be providing training targets for the combined nations honing their skills. Hopefully this will not occur, and China will show respect for and observance of the rights of free passage and the various economic zones. Indeed, China has as much at stake as any nation, increasingly dependent itself on the freedom of the seas for imported resources. Change for the better in East Asia has been illustrated by the transformation of Vietnam, a nation that at the conclusion of the Vietnam War could barely sustain its population at the poverty level. Today, it has rejected the Marxist-Leninist model and pursues a state capitalist economy. Nothing is more symbolic of change than the $1.3 billion investment made by Intel outside Ho Chi Minh City. Vietnam's 95.54 million people are now at a new level of prosperity and growth, perhaps unthinkable at the time of another symbolic memory, the last US helicopter departing the empty Saigon embassy in 1975. Vietnam can become a close ally and major trading partner with the United States and its Five Eyes allies, and be integrated with the other Asian nations in a new Asian maritime strategy. The United States and the United Kingdom with their Five Eyes intelligence allies should be strident in implementing the new strategy. It combines the maintaining of vital US and allied national interests, even to the extent of keeping the peace by preparing for war, with an internationalist maritime strategy that focuses on the enduring significance of the sea. The sea is both the means and the end in a modern US-UK and Five Eyes Asian strategy. Peace in the Indo-Pacific Region and the Relationship with India: Back in the 1960s US Secretary of State Dean Rusk advised President Kennedy that "India is key to countering China." The US went in an opposite direction, investing huge support across a broad spectrum of civil–military aid to Pakistan, driving India towards Russia for most of the Cold War, with the Soviet Union becoming India's chief arms supplier. Experience has shown that Pakistan cannot be trusted, in fact is duplicitous in many regards, as shown by the key Pakistani facility at Gwadar for China to have a naval base for the foreseeable future, with China now providing major arms supplies to Pakistan. US diplomacy with India has fortunately shown most positive signs. In 2015 President Obama issued a "US–India Joint Strategic Vision for the Asia–Pacific and the Indian Ocean region." On April 11, 2016 in the *Times* of India, US Secretary Ashton Carter wrote a key lead article entitled, "A Firm Strategic handshake: The India–US Partnership is moving to embrace defense tech transfers and maritime cooperation." On June 7, 2016 the White House issued a joint statement: "The United States and India: Enduring Global Partners in the21st century." All this was converted to hard legislative fact in the US Congress.

In 2016 India was formally declared a "Major Defense Partner" (MDP), and this was underwritten in the US Defense Authorization Act 2017, cementing the MDP into US law.15 The Asia Reassurance Act of 2018 further solidified this. On June 8,2016 Prime Minister Narendra Modi of India gave a groundbreaking "Address to a Joint Meeting of Congress." The so called "trust deficit" between India and the US that had persisted since the US–Pakistan alliance was slowly and effectively being eroded, though it is still not quite there. With a population in 2018 of 1,349,217, 956 (versus in China in 2019 1,409,517,397), India is not just the largest democracy in the world, it also faces off against a single party communist state that is now supporting India's chief political–military problem, Pakistan, exacerbated by China's presence next door in Gwadar, Pakistan. To overcome decades of US–India mistrust characterized by India's desire to both appear and actually to be nonaligned, India's sense of US diplomatic ambiguities, its own internal bureaucratic inertia and sense of not wanting to move into another quasi "colonial orbit," albeit it the United States, there has to be several years of confidence building. Intelligence can be key to this because India needs all the help it can get given the Kashmir scenario, and China's support for and alignment with Pakistan. A combination of intelligence cooperation and sharing, plus a steady increase in naval cooperation can go hand-in-hand. The two are complementary. In addition, the Five Eyes can extend intelligence relations beyond the maritime to assist India over its border disputes with Pakistan and likely Chinese operations with Pakistan against Indian key national security interests. The US Army and those of its Five Eyes allies may provide specialist technical support, complemented by ground, space, and other sources and methods that the Five Eyes have in spades. On the critical maritime scene Five Eyes navies can provide, over time, confidence- building intelligence support and across-the-board cooperation for both collection and analyses against China and its surrogates. The Indian Ocean is a maritime highway and the type of intelligence that the UK and US can provide with the other three nations will help India better define its future naval force structure and investment. This has to be an incremental confidence-building process because all those nations not aligned with either China or Russia will need a strong Indian Navy. It is likely that by the mid-2020s India will have a 160-ship navy that will include 3 aircraft carriers, 60 major surface combatants, and 400 aircraft. As a value of the Indian defense budget the navy will have increased from a mere 4% in 1960 to 8% in 1970, to 11% in 1992, and to 18% in 2009,16 and although this increase is laudable an even higher percentage will be required to take the Indian Navy from its sobriquet of the "Cinderella" service to the next level of operational performance so that it can operate unilaterally with the US Navy and multilaterally with the Five Eyes navies. This interoperability between navies will require establishing secure intelligence links, discreet encrypted communications, and critical data links such as Link 16, a tactical data link network used by NATO, and all the attendant satellite communication connections. Common seamanship standards and protocols such as replenishment at sea, vertical replenishment, ammunition replenishments, and a host of key seamanship drills and maneuvers will have to become ingrained as second nature in a new generation of Indian naval personnel. To underpin these developments India will need a "Grand Strategic" direction to enable the Indian Navy's future leadership and its political oversight to move in unison to reduce US–Indian political ambiguities, achieve expectation goals, and slowly move India into the realm as the major maritime power in the Indian Ocean. Assisting Indiawith the India–Pakistan scenario will help considerably through US mechanisms such as the Defense Technology and Trade Initiative (DTTI) to leverage for example US Special Forces and rapid reaction cell capabilities in India's border disputes. The sales of P-8 Poseidon maritime reconnaissance and ASW aircraft, SH-3 ASW helicopters, and aircraft carrier and jet engine technologies has helped reaffirm US commitment to India's growing navy. All this is good, and at the heart of change will be Five Eyes intelligence cooperation and collaboration. The Russia of Vladimir Putin:

Russia has clearly violated the norms of international behavior by its annexation of the Crimea and its invasion of Ukraine in February 2022. Russia's avowed objectives are not difficult to ascertain, whatever the pleadings of its leader. Without its oil and gas productions and the exports that flow from these, the Russian, economy would be in seriously worse shape than at present. The oligarchic nature of the Russian communist party, the roles of small controlling economic elites, and the Russian Mafia, plus the very nature of Vladimir Putin's background as a former KGB operative that makes him secretive and authoritarian, could add up to a recipe for long-term failure, particularly if at some point both the opposition groups and Russian masses coalesce into an effective alternative. The huge personal wealth accumulated by a tiny Russian minority must at some point come back to haunt them, but the exact nature and timing of such denouement are difficult to predict. Vladimir Putin's personal treasure trove cannot be ignored by the Russian people and web users indefinitely. However, the converse of this is a perpetual Putin led dictatorship with opposition groups stifled or worst case removed. How the Ukraine war impacts Putin's political survival remains to be seen. At the time of writing in early 2024, Putin faces multiple challenges. However, he oversees a dictatorial state with vast means of controls and security. Opponents are imprisoned. Two fundamental facts need to be stated. First, Russia's GDP, US$1,578 trillion in 2017–2018, is significantly less than that of the state of California, US$2.448 in 2015–2016. California had a population of 39.54 million in 2017, Russia 144.5 million in 2017.17 These core facts say an enormous amount. Second, Russia has nuclear weapons. Without these weapons readers are encouraged to assess for themselves where they think that Russia would be in the international order, notwithstanding that Russia is a member of the United Nations Security Council and has veto power. Without nuclear weapons, and its oil and gas, it is likely that Russia would not have a lead place in the international order for the foreseeable future, unless an alliance with China matures beyond oil deals between the two leaders of Russia and China. Combined Russian-Chinese operations in East Asia focusing on Japan and other nations may become a serious matter for concern. During the Cold War the Soviet Navy was a serious challenge. The whole NATO edifice kept the Soviet Navy in check by and large. However, we should also not that the Berlin Wall could not have come down soon enough, given the technical strides that the Soviets appeared to have been making, with their ship and submarine build rates most worrisome. Glasnost and Perestroika changed all that, with Mikhail Gorbachev becoming General Secretary of the Central Committee of the Communist Party of the Soviet Union in March 1985. How far Vladimir Putin wishes to put the clock back remains to be seen—indeed whether this is at all credible is an open question, given Russia's financial situation. On the strategic missile submarine side of the equation the Russians have, after moribund period following the collapse of the Soviet Union, begun a program to rebuild its SSBN Fleet, with four Borei-class SSBNs in the fleet and, according to the Russian News Agency Tass, another 11 expected to be built by 2020. The three remaining Delta III-class SSBNs and six Delta VI-class SSBNs will be gone from the inventory by the 2020s. The Russians are building the Yasen-class SSGN, with eight ordered so far, and an SSN class that is purported to begin building in 2016, with perhaps fifteen completed by 2035. News reports state that after the improved Kilo-class of six for the Black Sea Fleet is completed the Russians will build a new air independent improved Lada-class – perhaps 14–18 of these over a 15-year period, with most of the class commissioned in the 2020s. Safety is a huge issue. Since 2000 the Russians had seven major nuclear submarine accidents. The worst of these was the *Kursk* that exploded and sank with the loss of all hands. The nuclear incident in 2019 that killed a group of senior Russian scientists is still being analyzed at the time of writing though it is suspected that a test nuclear propulsion unit became out of control. Russia's submarine force, until the recent resurgence, was older than 30 years. However, by positioning its remaining more capable submarines and new SSNs and SSBNs, together with its nuclear-capable bombers and land-based missiles, Putin's Russia can send unfavorable messages to the West, for example, moving nuclear weapons near to the Polish border, and certainly moving nuclear weapons into the Crimea during the current conflict will be seen by NATO as an aggressive act. The sustainment of US-UK Intelligence with full Five Eyes intelligence support is crucial in this environment to support NATO. The Russian surface navy is not in good shape, much worse than perhaps media sources relate, with perhaps too grandiose plans for possible aircraft carriers, frigates, corvettes, and large destroyers on the order of 15,000 tons, together with a cruiser modernization program for the Kirov- and Slava-classes, and the Udaloy destroyers, though the *Sovremennyy*-class destroyers will be retired. In spite of the French Mistral class amphibious ship debacle, it looks like the Russians may build two to three 14,000–16,000-ton amphibious ships, and four *Ivan Gren*-class amphibious ships in each of the Black Sea and Baltic Fleets. All of the above is very much dependent on both Russian yard capacity and finances. If all the above happened by about 2030 the Russian navy could in effect be back in serious business. The question for US-UK Intelligence is: is this at all achievable? To date unclassified Five Eyes data shows that the Russians have fallen behind almost every program with delays and major difficulties. The overall picture is reasonably clear: the Russian Navy will concentrate on strategic deterrence, the SSBN force, and coastal defense, with the blue water navy of the Cold War era still to be determined. Russian incursions, for example, near to UK air space are by relatively aging moribund aircraft and have the aura of defunct Cold War saber rattling to very little effect. The question for the West and specifically US-UK Intelligence is how to counter and modify Russian aggressive moves, short of direct confrontation. Where, for example, does the maritime mix play in this? Sanctions and diplomacy have impacted Russia, though the former have negative economic connotations for the West, particularly the European nations dependent on Russian energy sources. Germany has made it very clear to both its EU partners and the United States that it needs Russian gas and the undersea gas pipeline from Russia to Germany is the critical infrastructure. The clandestine attack on the Russian undersea pipeline in the Baltic Sea polarized the criticality of Russian supplied gas, and especially its significant contribution to the Russian economy. The Ukraine war brought this sharply into focus. The US argument that Germany could be held hostage to Russian supply is countered by those analysts that argue that Putin's Russia desperately needs the income from German gas sales, and that the relationship is complementary, not potentially an economic hostage situation. The Ukraine war has changed the dynamics of this. Russia is now in 2024 busily finding other buyers of Russian energy, and China is clearly a major customer. Russia has found surrogates to circumvent sanctions imposed as a consequence of its invasion of Ukraine. Naval power in both the Baltic and Black Seas, judiciously applied with the forward-deployed allied presence of multi-national naval forces, together with classical diplomacy, can send a clear message that aggression will not be rewarded. A US Navy and US Marine Corps MEF (Marine Expeditionary Force)-level surge into either or both seas, supported by the NATO navies, and supported by all elements of the Five Eyes intelligence community, sends not just a clear message of intent and deterrence. It shows solidarity of purpose and the clear military ability to stop aggression in its tracks. The Russian invasion of Ukraine, and a worst-case threat to NATO allies in the Baltic States, can be met with an unequivocal display of overwhelming naval and marine/amphibious power. US and other key NATO forces can display, by forward deployed and persistent presence, a similar capability that was shown, for instance, at Inchon in the Korean War. A large and flexible amphibious force that is deployed from the sea, at short notice, with no requirements for shore support, can send a key message, along with diplomacy, in support of the allied cause.

This involves therefore the classic display of naval expeditionary warfare based on three main tenets: forward-persistent presence, flexibility to use those forces in terms of the mix and combination of naval forces, and maneuver from the sea at a time and places of one's choosing. These abiding principles will be underpinned by US-UK and Five Eyes intelligence sources and methods, indicators and warnings, and collective sustained analysis. The psychological make up of our adversaries and those who wish the United Kingdom and the United States and their allies' ill intent is a critical component of any analysis of their plans and operations. Intelligence that ignores or does not include such analysis is likely built on shifting sand. In the contemporary content take the classic example of Vladimir Putin. Vladimir Putin is a Yuri Andropo lookalike, with Andropov later attaining the General Secretaryship of the Soviet Communist Party, not unlike how Putin acceded to power. Everything Putin thinks and does is characterized by his KGB beginnings, his training, his actions, and therefore how he can be predicted to behave. This is vital in any US-UK intelligence assessment of Russian intentions, plans, and operations. Personality is critical. We should look at Russia through the Putin lens and that of his key oligarchs. The Five Eyes and allies have to understand and analyze the inner mindset of Putin and his FSB operatives, his oligarchic friends, his security system, his deception techniques, and his electronic eavesdropping capabilities and procedures, of which cyber penetration for example of the US 2016 election, is merely one amongst many. He and his closest staff, plus the trusted foot soldiers that make up Putin's coterie and do the real work on the ground, always have a strategy and plan. Unraveling that strategy and plan is step one. It is clear to the layperson that Putin very much wants sanctions lifted with the West and, at a more grandiose level, he has a desire to restore mother Russia to another level of recognition and self-aggrandizement for himself, at the expense whenever and wherever possible of what he sees as the old adversaries in NATO and their associated allies. Vladimir Putin sees the Five Eyes as adversaries. The secret of Putin's success, as most likely measured by his criteria and KGB/

FSB standards, is to be not directly exposed to direct evidence of his personal involvement in Russian intelligence operations. Putin's operatives' trade craft is not to communicate while others listen, to launder money through multiple channels with no traceable fingerprints, to hold several passports and identities, to always guard their back and personal weaknesses whenever possible, and to disarm and dissemble with consummate urbanity. This is what the FSB and its surrogates in both the Russian mafia and the wealthy oligarchs are very simply all about. The cultural and historical underpinnings are all there to be analyzed. The psychological make-up of the Russian leader and his immediate entourage holds the key to predicting Russian policies and their likely outcomes. There is clear and perceptible lineal descent at one level from the post-World War II Soviet leadership to Vladimir Putin. The lives and careers of Georgy Malenkov, Nikita Khrushchev Leonid Brezhnev, Yuri Andropov, Konstantin Chernenko, to the great change brought about by Mikhail Gorbachev, reveal aspects of their mindsets, behavior, and policies that enabled us to predict with reasonable accuracy their likely reaction to changing global geo-strategic realities in the context of domestic Soviet politics and economics. The same applies to Vladimir Putin and his regime. US-UK Intelligence will be able to unravel many of Putin authorized asymmetric and apparently non state sponsored covert operations and cyber space initiatives by examining both his past and current dependence on means that run contrary to the maintenance of international order. Putin is not difficult to predict. The secret for US-UK Intelligence is to penetrate and contain the operations generated by this old-style KGB operative who has grasped the significance of the digital era. Hopefully the Ukraine invasion will be Putin's fatal mistake. Time will tell. In January, 2024 the war is still in progress.

Collection and Analysis:

In some instances, the past may remain prologue in terms of the collection technologies and assessments that were employed successfully during the Cold War being applied to emerging post 2020 military threat systems of potential aggressor states. This is particularly true of ELINT and MASINT collection against new systems and technologies, and to assess when they will gain initial operational capability (IOC) as they appear from the production lines of China, Russia, North Korea, Iran, and, to some extent, Israel. It is salutatory to recall that Israel supplied Argentina with various key military assets both during and after the Falklands conflict. For example, after the conflict Israel refitted three Boeing 707 aircraft with advanced SIGINT equipment that was clearly not in the best interests of the Five Eyes community. The counterintelligence services of all the Five Eyes monitor commercial and military technology gathering by Israel and its surrogates and technical representatives, knowing that Israel has commercial and financial interests in understanding and garnering the latest Western technologies that it can use in its own industrial base. The motive is very simply economic wellbeing that is not unreasonable, except that it involves in essence taking Five Eyes technology, reproducing it, and then selling on the international markets Of course, China and Russia are much bigger and more serious targets for counterintelligence against classical technical espionage as well as perfectly legal acquisition of Western technology by surrogate means. The open societies of the Five Eyes are much more vulnerable than the closed and heavily secret and pervasive societies of China, Russia, North Korea, and Iran, where human rights have no legal standing. Penetration of programs in the very early stages of R&D through initial design and production of emerging advanced technologies in threat countries will require new and innovative collection methodologies. Take for example the development of hypervelocity weapons with speeds and ranges not contemplated during the Cold War. Similarly, with situational awareness, targeting, and space systems technologies, where there is in the case of the latter a growing need to deploy defensive counterspace systems because of adversary offensive counter space systems. The Five Eyes require more resilient and defendable space assets. Similarly with networked, AI-intensive, and fully integrated advanced UUV (Unmanned Underwater Vehicle) and UAV/UCAS systems there will be major requirements to use the latest AI tools to enhance real-time intelligence collection and secure distribution without any possibility of interception and/or jamming. All major threats see Five Eyes space assets as huge threats to their ability to cover-up technical developments, initial testing, and then deployment. For instance, Five Eyes advanced space-based infrared systems have the capability to unmask myriad different threat developments. As AI becomes more and more commonplace within the interlaced Five Eyes collection networks the overall ability of the major threats will be increasingly fraught to deceive and surprise. GPS vulnerability has been an issue for many years. Between October 16 and November 7, 2018 it was alleged by the Norwegian Ministry of Defense that the Russian military jammed NATO GPS signals during the largest NATO military exercise since the Cold War, Trident Juncture, in Norway, that involved 50,000 US and NATO forces. Jamming evidently occurred in the Kola Peninsula. None of this is surprising, and of course it does tip NATO's hand to what the threat constitutes. I was shown in 2018 and held a GPS jamming device manufactured in China that could jam local commercial GPS signals within about a 10-mile radius. This is daunting if such devices are in the wrong hands, whether criminals, terrorists, malcontents, mentally unstable persons, or worst-case intelligence agents and deep-rooted undercover plants awaiting instructions in the event of hostilities. In 2013, a New Jersey man bought an illegal GPS jammer to thwart the tracking device in his company vehicle. His GPS jammer, bought online for less than $100, interfered with a new GPS guidance system called Smartpath being tested at Newark Liberty airport. Federal agents tracked his jamming signal to his truck. He received a very heavy fine, as well as losing his job.19

In the past seven years since the incident above, jamming technology has improved considerably. Military- and intelligence-grade jammers are in a league of their own from commercially accessible devices. US-UK Intelligence has the capability to collectively design and employ the most advanced anti-jam GPS devices that will undoubtedly both confuse and deceive the threat, while indeed homing weapons onto the source. The essential parameters of electronic warfare persist. Those who seek to do bad things with what may appear to be state-of-the-art offensive tools often become their own worst enemy. Modern HUMINT:

Perhaps the single biggest challenge facing those who manage clandestine HUMINT operations in the digital era is how to securely and covertly maintain contact with HUMINT sources without counterintelligence services detecting an agent. This is an important task. In the digital era counterintelligence agencies have become adept at intercepting the discreet communications of those who are betraying their nations' secrets, however disguised and buried such communications may be. Classical dead letter drops and meetings that involve an agent avoiding counterintelligence followers are most likely a thing of the past and spy novels. Sheer physical access in such countries as North Korea and Iran is hugely challenging. Contacts are most likely to be made at official functions. The problem even in these situations where US-UK Intelligence operatives have diplomatic status, is that the counterintelligence services of host nations will be fully active. They will be watching, listening, and videoing the activities of their nationals as they have iterations with diplomats, trade negotiators, visiting senior business executives, academic researchers, and so on. A report that was issued in Yahoo News on November 2, 2018 by two capable investigative journalists, Zach Dorman and Jenna McLaughlin, illustrates the above. They discovered that the CIA's internet-based communications system for covert exchanges with overseas agents was compromised. This happened between 2009–2013, with the compromise initiated in Iran. They state: "More than two dozen sources died in China in 2011 and 2012 as a result, according to 11 former intelligence and national security officials," evidently disclosed under the apparent protection of anonymity. They continued: "The issue was that it (the communications system) was working well for too long with too many people. But it was an elementary system." According to their sources Iran succeeded in breaking up a CIA HUMINT network that hampered US intelligence collection against Iran's nuclear program. Dorman and McLaughl in state: "Two former US intelligence officials said that the Iranians cultivated a double agent who led them to the secret CIA communications system." The system was an online system. We are led to believe that once the Iranian double agent revealed to Iran's counterintelligence people the website, the Iranians then scoured the webfor other likely operatives, revealing "who in Iran was visiting these sites, and from where, and began to unravel the wider CIA network." In May 2017 the *New York Times* reported the loss of 30 CIA agents in China, and in May 2018 CIA officer Jerry Lee, based in Beijing, was charged with spying for the Chinese. *Foreign Policy* magazine reported that, "Chinese intelligence broke through the firewall separating it (CIA communications system) from the main covert communications system, compromising the CIA's entire asset network in that country." One may conclude that perhaps China and Iran cooperated in these events. Whatever the accuracy of the above claims, one fact is significant and has been verified. Back in 2008 a defense contractor named John Reidy blew the whistle on various inadequacies and vulnerabilities after his management would not listen this technical concerns. His complaints were not adequately addressed, and he was fired from his position in November 2011. He had assessed that about 70% of CIA covert operations were compromised. One may speculate that if Reidy's concerns had been addressed early enough then lives could have been saved. Running Covert Agents: What these unclassified public reports illustrate is simply that running covert agents has never been more difficult than today and in the future, even in the case of the classic "walk-ins" where prospective agents visit Five Eyes diplomatic facilities ormake contact with an official in order to start a dialogues of betraying their nations' secrets. Such facilities and overt US-UK Intelligence personnel in sensitive overseas cities such as Moscow, Beijing, Tehran, and Pyongyang are so heavily monitored by multiple surveillance systems and human assets that any individual entering or meeting with a foreign official is likely to be immediately identified. Perhaps long gone are the days when a key MI6 agent from the Cold War, Oleg Gordievsky, a senior KGB official who became head of the KGB (Rezident or station chief) in the London Rezidentura (station) may be recruited by direct contact under the eyes of Soviet counterintelligence. Ben Macintyre's fine book, *The Spy and the Traitor*, spells out in detail how MI6 recruited and ran Gordievsky until he was betrayed by no other than CIA's traitor, Aldrich Ames, as a result of his boss's security complacency and indiscretions. All the above calls into question the future value of HUMINT. US-UK Intelligence however has enormous combined strategic leverage when it comes to HUMINT, assuming that one avoids the notion that all HUMINT is about covert and clandestine agent-running. The enormous bandwidth of the digital era combined with international travel across every part of human endeavor means that there are new and challenging ways to exploit old-fashioned classical HUMINT. HUMINT is by no means dead, and it will take on new forms based on advanced technology, ingenuity, and innovation for which Bletchley Park forebears would be justly proud. A new generation of original thinkers within US-UK Intelligence can indeed revolutionize HUMINT in unprecedented ways.

Climate Change

Climate change has to be a concern for US-UK Intelligence. The US and the UK with their many allies and friendly nations are together spending billions on national defense while our planet is threatened by the undeniable scientific evidence of climate change. The question is, will the international community, and their intelligence communities specifically, be able to mobilize resources to counter this threat. The cascading effects of climate change are predicted to destabilize highly vulnerable regions and tens, and likely hundreds, of millions of people, including for example large centers of urban population in the United States. The United States walked away from the 2015 Paris Climate Agreement. This has been rectified by the Biden Administration. Without United States' leadership and investment in countering the effects of climate change there is a huge international gap, a task that the Five Eyes community as a whole needs to address. What is the key scientific evidence? The glaciers in Antarctica and the Himalaya mountains are melting and these effects alone will significantly impact our planet. The melting Thwaites Glacier in Antarctica is the size of Florida and if it melts completely scientists estimate that global ocean levels will rise by 2 feet. January 2019 was the hottest month ever recorded in Australia, with 2017 and 2018 the hottest years ever recorded. Rising temperatures are estimated to melt one third of the glaciers in the Hindu Kush region of the Himalayas.20 National security and climate change are inextricably linked. The US Department of Defense includes climate change in its threat data and analytics, while conversely the Trump White House challenged the global scientific community. This has fortunately been rectified. The United States' Director of National Intelligence has stated that, "Global environmental and ecological degradation, as well as climate change, are likely to fuel competition for resources, economic distress, and social discontent." What is clearly required is international commitment and agreement, and for the US-UK Intelligence community and Five Allies to make a stand through technical intelligence support and do what the late Carl Sagan advocated, to stand together and, "Preserve and cherish the pale blue dot, the only home we've ever known." Drastic change will be needed, and US-UK Intelligence will become critical by using the vast array of technical intelligence tools to collect and analyze data in the service of the planet. A Five Eyes summit led by the US and the UK will have to continuously monitor and address how each nation can contribute to economic intelligence collection and analysis, together with the impact of climate change.

APPENDIX B

INFLUENTIAL INDIVIDUALS AND MENTORS

Royal Navy Admiral Sir Reginald "Blinker" Hall

The Zimmermann Telegram was one of the greatest intelligence triumphs of British history. Its centenary was commemorated in 2017—and it is most important to recognize the continuity of events since 1917. The Royal Navy Admiral Sir Reginald "Blinker" Hall was the architect of this most famous intelligence coup of all time. He was called "Blinker" because of a permanent facial twitch that he exploited with characteristic aplomb. Hall's genius lay in his early and extraordinarily successful exploitation of radio telegraphy and its cryptologic underpinnings. Hall did not know this at the time, but his actions and those of his key subordinates set the stage for arguably saving the civilized world from tyranny in the Nazi era as a result of critical intelligence cooperation and sharing of the most sensitive secrets. The Five Eyes owe much to Admiral Sir Reginald Blinker Hall. Without the foundations built by him and the maintenance of inter-war capabilities, in spite of the financial downturn caused by the Great Depression, it is difficult to see how the British would have established by 1939 at Bletchley Park what would become a highly secret war-winning organization, working in total cooperation with the US Office of Naval Intelligence. Blinker Hall was the son of the first director of British Naval Intelligence,

William Henry Hall, so intelligence was in his blood when he entered the Royal Navy in 1884. As a captain, Blinker Hall was the DNI throughout World War I, and because of his huge successes he was promoted to rear admiral in 1917, after the Zimmermann Telegram. Later he became vice admiral, 1922, and admiral, 1926. The British Naval Intelligence Department (NID) was created in 1887, with mainly the defense of British imperial trade interests as a primary driver. In 1887 there were a mere ten staff officers with a budget of about 5,000 pounds a year. Many in the Royal Navy leadership were against such a staff, with senior officers such as Admiral Fisher disclaiming in no uncertain terms that a staff would, "convert splendid sea officers into very indifferent clerks." When Hall became the DNI, and war was declared in August 1914 he faced much intransigence characterized by a combination of prejudice and ignorance. Operational intelligence as we understand it today was primitive to nonexistent. Hall took one extraordinary step that was to revolutionize naval warfare and which, with the benefit of hindsight today, may seem obvious, but in 1914 was clouded in fog. Hall realized that exploitation of wireless telegraphy and its cryptography could be war winners, what modern parlance would characterize as technical game changers. Hall built wisely on the work of Sir Alfred Ewing, a professor of Mechanical Engineering at Cambridge, who was brought into the Admiralty as the Director of Naval Education and then created the first ever cipher team. Hall's "Room 40" became the heart and soul of naval intelligence in World War I, building on Ewing's foundations, to create a cadre of first-class cryptographers. Hall's single biggest problem was interfacing with the Operations Division of the Admiralty where there was institutional bias against new and mainly civilian technical experts advising operators on key intelligence from wireless intercepts. The issue was clear to Hall: the operators did not wish to share their operational data with Room 40 civilian cryptographers and the latter were deprived of the key opportunity to both analyze and interpret cryptographic intelligence in light of current and planned British naval operations and, most of all, their German adversaries. This failure to make the wise use of such intelligence reached its nadir at Jutland, a subject that has been much underrated in understanding why Jutland was not the success that the Royal Navy wanted and the country expected. So, what did Hall get up to between January and March 1917 that will forever live in the annals of any intelligence organization worldwide and provided a blueprint for Five Eyes intelligence much later? First, the overall political–military context inwhich Hall and his Room 40 team were operating. The United States was not in the war in January 1917. The Germans were planning on restarting unrestricted U-boat warfare from February 1, 1917 in an attempt to bring the British economy to its knees by attacking its most vital national interest, seaborne trade. This one fact could be the tipping point for the American President to convince his people to join the war on the Allied side, remembering that in the United States in 1917 anti-British sentiment ran high, with a volatile and outspoken Irish-American and German-American population. Second, on January 11, 1917, the German Foreign Minister, Arthur Zimmermann, presented an encoded telegram to the US Ambassador in Berlin, James W. Gerard, who agreed to transmit the telegram in its coded form. The American Embassy transmitted this telegram on January 16, 1917, five days later. Why would the German Foreign Ministry be using the American Embassy to send its messages, in this case (the Zimmermann Telegram) via Washington DC to the German Ambassador in Mexico City, Heinrich von Eckhardt? Hall and his staff had realized very early on that undersea communications cables could provide the source of great intelligence and also that by denying their use by cable cutting, an enemy could be deprived of vital communications. The British had cut the German transatlantic cable at the beginning of the war in 1914. The US was neutral in 1914 and permitted Germany limited use of its Europe to US transatlantic cable mainly because President Woodrow Wilson was encouraging peace talks and wanted to ensure that Berlin could talk with the US diplomatically. Zimmermann's telegram was instructing the German Ambassador in Mexico City to inform the Mexican President, Carranza, that if the US entered the war against Germany then Germany would support Mexico financially in fighting a war against the US to regain territory lost to Mexico in the wars with the United States, a bombshell of enormous proportions if made aware to the US government and people. Hall's Room 40 was reading all the American traffic (that ran via cable from the US embassy in Denmark), including all German traffic, encrypted or otherwise, that was forwarded from the US Embassy in Berlin. The US cable went via the UK, and the intercept point was at a relay station at Porthcurno, near Land's End. Hall's civilian cryptographers Nigel de Grey and William Montgomery brilliantly decrypted the Zimmermann telegram the following day after interception by the British on January 17, 1917. Why was this so speedy and efficient? Hall and his team had also pulled off two critical earlier coups. Room 40 had captured secretly during the Mesopotamian campaign the German Diplomatic Cipher 13040 and, as a result of very good clandestine relations with the Russians, Hall obtained the critical German Naval Cipher 0075 (the 007 part will not be lost on readers). The Russians had obtained this from the German cruiser *Magdeburg* after it was wrecked. Hall had secretly nursed Russian relations. The genius of Hall was what he did and did not do next. The Americans may well think that this was all a devious British plot to bring the United States into the war. The telegram was brutally explicit in two regards: on February 1, 1917 the Germans would resume unrestricted U-boat warfare, and a German–Mexican military alliance was proposed, with Germany as the funding source. Hall needed a cover story for his knowledge of the German codes and to avoid the Americans knowing that Room 40 was reading their and others' mail, while at the same time convincing Woodrow Wilson and his government that the telegram was real, not a British forgery. Hall never once consulted anyone in the British Foreign Office or within the Admiralty Staff. He acted with his staff alone. He then decided on his "deception plan." This was the real genius of this extraordinary brilliant work by Hall and his team. Hall knew one key fact: the German Embassy in Washington DC, once it received the telegram, would have to transmit it to the

German Embassy in Mexico City. Hall knew that they used a commercial telegraph company. NID agents bribed a Mexican telegraph employee to yield the cipher, thereby enabling Hall to inform the Americans that this had come directly from the Mexican Telegraph company from Washington DC. Simple, but brilliant. Hall also, in parallel, took another quite remarkable action, by great timing, by doing nothing until the Germans announced unrestricted U-Boar warfare on February 1, 1917, after which the US broke off diplomatic relations with Germany on February 3, 1917. Hall then did two key things. He only informed the British Foreign Secretary on February 5, 1017 with an emphatic request that the British Foreign Office delay all diplomatic moves with the US until Hall himself took various actions. With Foreign Office knowledge, Hall then met with the Secretary of the US Embassy in London, Edward Bell, on February 19, 1917, and the following day Hall met with the US Ambassador to the Court of St. James, Walter Hines Page, and handed him the telegram. Three days later Ambassador Page met with the British Foreign Secretary, Arthur Balfour, and on Hall's quite emphatic advice he gave the American ambassador a copy of the stolen Mexican cipher text and the English translation of the full Zimmermann telegram. After some analysis and discussion in Washington, President Wilson was convinced. He went ahead and released the telegram to the US press on February 28, 1917, and this immediately inflamed American public opinion against both Germany and Mexico. Wilson and his top aides realized also that they had to protect the British "Mexican cipher" and British code-breaking capabilities. Herein lay the foundations of what became years later the beginning of what Humphrey Bogart, playing Rick Blaine, said at the very end of the 1942 movie *Casablanca* to Claude Rains, playing the cynical French police chief Captain Louis Renault: "Louis, I think this is the beginning of a beautiful friendship." The American protection of Britain's secrets was indeed the beginning of a very special relationship. Further positive news for Hall and his Room 40 team was that the Mexican President had been advised that German funding was unreliable, and that a successful war with the

United States was unlikely. President Venustiano Carranza was also advised that even if German funding did materialize their sister South American nations, Argentina, Brazil, and Chile, from whom Mexico would purchase arms, would likely be unsupportive of a Mexican alliance with Germany and a war with the United States. Nonetheless the Mexican government did not enforce an embargo against Germany, much to the chagrin of the United States, and Mexico continued to do business with Germany throughout World War I. However, Mexico did not repeat history in World War II, declaring war on the Axis Powers on May 22, 1942. The final coup de grace was delivered by none other than Arthur Zimmermann himself, who rashly announced on March 3, 1917, in a press conference, that the telegram was in fact true. He then very naively followed this with a statement in the Reichstag on March 29, 1917 that his plan had been for Germany to fund Mexico only if the Americans declared war on Germany. The United States Congress declared war on Germany on April 6, 1917, President Wilson having asked for this declaration on April 2, 1917. Hall and his Room 40 team had triumphed, and Hall was promoted to Rear Admiral shortly thereafter The significance of Hall's achievements and relationship with his American counterparts has to be put in context, 103 years later in 2020. The US Ambassador in London, Walter Hines Page (August 15, 1855–December 21, 1918) described Blinker Hall as the single most influential person, indeed genius, of World War I. There is a memorial plaque in honor of Walter Hines Page in Westminster Abbey, in Westminster, London. He and Hall had a special relationship that bound both the United Kingdom and the United States forever in sharing sensitive intelligence.

Sir Michael Howard

After school at Wellington College and Christ Church, Oxford, Michael Howard(1922–) served in the Coldstream Guards in the Italian campaign, winning the Military Cross for gallantry at the first battle of Monte Cassino in 1944. He founded the Department of

War Studies at King's College London, as a lowly assistant lecturer and by the sheer weight of outstanding research and teaching, plus energetic and persistent leadership, grew a formidable but in those days a small department. He left, just as I joined King's, to become successively at Oxford the Chichele Professor of the History of War and, from 1980–1989, the ultimate accolade of Regius Professor of Modern History, succeeding Professor Hugh Trevor-Roper (later Lord Dacre), the famous author of the best-selling *The Last Days of Hitler*. Michael Howard completed his active academic career in the United States, as the Robert A. Lovett Professor of Military and Naval History at Yale from 1989 to 1993. As a schoolboy at Bablake I had read his *The Franco-Prussian War of 1870–71* and even then at a young age I had appreciated his mastery of not just detail but the exquisite nature of his analysis and language. As I started research at King's the turnover was in progress with his successor, Professor Sir Laurence Martin (born 1928), who had studied at Christ's College, Cambridge, and Yale University. He spent ten years at King's before becoming Vice Chancellor of Newcastle University in 1978 and then Director of Chatham House, the Royal Institute of International Affairs, in 1991. I got on very well with Laurence Martin. I liked his "American approach" to defense and intelligence and as my research took shape he rapidly realized, as did I, that others needed to become closely involved.

Bryan Ranft

I first had contact with Professor Bryan Ranft at the Royal Naval College, Greenwich, where he was head of Naval History and International Affairs. Bryan was a World War II veteran like Michael Howard, a Manchester Grammar School and Balliol College, Oxford, graduate before World War II broke out. At Balliol he was a contemporary of Denis Healey (1917–2015) who became Secretary of State for Defence, 1964–1970, Chancellor of the Exchequer, 1974–1979, and finally Deputy Leader of the Labor Party from 1980–1983. Like Ranft, Healey served in the

British Army in World War II from 1940–1945, reaching the rank of major in the Royal Engineers in the North Africa Campaign, Italian Campaign, and at the battle of Anzio. Healey came from modest beginnings and won a scholarship to Balliol College from Bradford Grammar School. At Oxford, Healey was a member of the Communist Party from 1937–1940, leaving the party when France fell to the Nazis. Healey was an outstanding Oxford scholar, gaining a "Double First" degree in 1940. At Balliol, besides Bryan Ranft, he became a lifelong friend and political rival of the future Conservative Prime Minister, Edward Heath, whom he succeeded as President of the Balliol Junior Common Room. Bryan Ranft's Oxford DPhil thesis had been on the protection of seaborne trade, a brilliant study that traced the early origins in fine detail of how Britain had successively pursued a maritime strategy primarily focused on the defense of trade. Ranft and Healey came to serious intellectual blows during Healey's tenure of the Ministry of Defence, with Healey laying the grounds for the serious reduction in the size, shape, capabilities, and deployment of the Royal Navy. He canceled the aircraft carrier replacement program, thus ending effectively Royal Navy fixed-wing aviation once the last of the fleet carriers was decommissioned. Overseas bases were to be closed and the Royal Navy was to be withdrawn from persistent forward presence in the Far East and Mediterranean to become a North-East Atlantic Navy. There were serious budgetary issues that Healey faced, but Ranft argued that strategically his policies were unbalanced, with over emphasis on the British Army of the Rhine comitments to the Central Front in Europe that many naval experts argued was unnecessary given the massive commitment by the US Army and the US Air Force, and underpinned by NATO's ability (read the United States) to use tactical nuclear weapons if the Red Army and its Warsaw Pact allies attempted to cross the FEBA (Forward Edge of the Battle Area). Ranft stated in several eloquently argued papers that Soviet expansionism and aggressive posturing was happening at sea, with Sovier Admiral Sergey Gorshkov (1910–1988) supported by the Soviet leadership following a classical maritime strategy to pursue the vital national interests of the Soviet Union. Time would prove Ranft completely correct, but it was too late to undo the severe damage that Healey did to the force structure and therefore deployability of the Royal Navy. Bryan Ranft rapidly realized that my research interests had polarized on a major unexplored topic in the late 1960s, which may seem unusual today with the total benefit of hindsight. I had been inspired and energized by both my work on the Nazi era and also my intense interest in naval warfare and how intelligence had played a crucial role in the allied victory at sea in Europe and the Pacific. Bryan Ranft was indeed a wonderfully kindly man and generous human being.

Sir Harry Hinsley

Hinsley was born in Walsall in the English Midlands November 26, 1918, and died in Cambridge on February 16, 1998, aged 79, from lung cancer. He came from modest beginnings and was clearly gifted intellectually. Contrary to popular misconceptions of lack of opportunity for working-class children in the 1930s in what is often characterized as a class-ridden society, the young Harry won a place at Queen Mary's Grammar School in Walsall. In 1937 Hinsley won a distinguished scholarship to read History at St. John's College, Cambridge. He was an outstanding scholar at Cambridge, rewarded years later in 1985 by his election to a Fellowship of the British Academy (FBA). When war was declared by Neville Chamberlainon September 3, 1939 after the September 1, 1939 invasion of Poland by Nazi Germany, the Government Code and Cipher School at Bletchley Park was seeking the best and brightest minds to meet the Nazi challenge. He was interviewed by the Director of Bletchley Park, the legendary Commander Alexander "Alastair" Deniston, Royal Navy (December 1, 1881–January 1, 1961) and was very soon thereafter working in "Hut 4," a location that decades later, not until the late 1970s/early 1980s in fact, would become synonymous with war-winning code breaking. Hut 4 provided the keys to critical successful operations against the Nazis and their allies, particularly in the hugely successful fight against the U-boats and helping the winning of the battle of the Atlantic by the most secretive clandestine means. Winston Churchill knew that without the maintenance of seaborne trade between the United States and the United Kingdom the British war effort could die a painful death. His wartime speeches reflect this harsh reality. At Bletchley Hinsley became intimately involved in parallel efforts in the United States, and particularly with the US Office of Naval Intelligence (ONI). Deniston recognized Hinsley's intellectual talent, together with other Bletchley luminaries such as Alan Turing and Gordon Welchman. In late 1943 Hinsley was in Washington DC, still a relatively young man, negotiating a highly classified SIGINT agreement with the United States. Towards the end of the war he was working for Sir Edward Travis, KCMG, CBE, (September 24, 1888–April 23, 1956), who was the operational head of Bletchley Park during World War II and later the head of Bletchley's successor, GCHQ. Travis was a critical person at Bletchley. He had joined the Royal Navy in 1906 as a Paymaster officer and served in HMS *Iron Duke*. Between 1916–1918 he worked in the famous Room 40 under Captain Blinker Hall. In 1925 Travis became Denniston's Deputy at the GC&CS. During World War II Travis became a critical player at Bletchley Park, about which much has been written in multiple books. Travis was instrumental in the signing of the 1943 UK–US .BR USA Agreement and the subsequent 1946 highly classified secret intelligence agreement, cementing the special relationship in the post-war period and laying the way for the creation of the Five Eyes intelligence agreements and the longest lasting intelligence cooperation in history. Travis was knighted in June 1944, though the reasons for his knighthood were cloaked in disarming secrecy. On paper it looked as if he was rewarded for diplomatic services which, at one level, he indeed had been.

By war's end, after distinguished work, for which he was made an Officer of the Order of the British Empire (OBE) in 1946, and having married the lady who he met at Bletchley Park, Hilary

Brett-Smith, Harry Hinsley was back at Cambridge, elected as a Fellow of St. John's College in 1945. In 1969, when I began work with him, he had recently been elected Professor of International Relations, having published earlier in 1962 his major work, *Power and the Pursuit of Peace*1 that was acclaimed internationally and sealed his academic reputation. His work on the official history of British intelligence in World War II changed dramatically the world view of historians, analysts, the media, current intelligence agencies and their employees, and the retired and serving military. His 1985 knighthood as justly deserved. He enjoyed the fruits of his labors and retirement from 1989, when he retired as Master of St. John's College, Cambridge, until his passing in February 1998, at age 79. The one accolade I sought came on December6, 1972 when I was awarded the degree of Doctor of Philosophy by the University of London, King's College.

Harry Hinsley, Sir Edward Travis, and John Titman in Washington

Vice Admiral Sir Norman "Ned" Denning

One of the finest people that I was privileged to meet on a regular basis was retired Vice Admiral Sir Norman "Ned" Denning (1904–1979). He had been a member of the famous "Room 39" during World War II, and later in his career Director of Naval Intelligence (1960–1964), Deputy Chief of the Defense Staff for Intelligence (1964–1967), and earlier 1956–1958 he held a senior position at Greenwich. I first met Admiral Denning through Bryan Ranft after the admiral had retired and was head of the famous "Defense and Security Media Advisory Board" or better known as the "D Notices Committee." The latter was the key committee that ensured that the British media did not unwittingly betray the UK's secrets via inadvertent news media. It meant that Admiral Denning had daily direct working relations with all the Fleet Street newspaper editors, the heads of the independent TV networks and the BBC, together with any other source that may give away information detrimental to national security. I met with Admiral Denning regularly. He gave me unfettered access to his incredible experience and memory bank that was truly prodigious. His career had spanned the greatest war in the history of our planet through to the Cold War. I soaked up his stories, his insights, his anecdotes, and most of all his wisdom. We would meet for about two hours at a time, often followed by lunch It was a huge privilege. Admiral Denning was also the brother of Lord Justice Alfred Thompson "Tom Denning (1899–1999), the Master of the Rolls (1962–1982), who Margaret Thatcher described as, "Probably the greatest English judge of modern times." Lord Denning joined Lincoln's Inn in 1921, and was called to the Bar in June 1923, a distinguished graduate of Magdalen College, Oxford. I have been a barrister of Lincoln's Inn, called in November 1980, almost 40 years ago at the time of writing, so by a wonderful quirk or irony of fate I was privileged to know both of these brothers, who came from modest beginnings and ascended to the highest offices in the UK, belying any notion that Britain was a class-ridden society in the early and mid-20th century.

James McConnell

During my second year at Greenwich, my colleagues and I, both uniformed teaching personnel and civilian academics, welcomed an American who came to us from the US National Security Agency and the US Navy's key think tank, the Center for Naval Analyses, or CNA for short. This gentleman was James "Jamie" McConnell, an extraordinarily capable and well-established Soviet Union intelligence analyst, and a specialist on all things Soviet Navy. Jamie was a Columbia University graduate in Russian. He was now the only person at Greenwich who not only spoke fluent Russian, and could read the subtle nuances of Soviet military and strategic thought, he was the ultimate expert on Russian open sources and knew in great detail what these were, how to obtain them, and most of all to interpret these sources against the highly classified intelligence sources, particularly SIGINT and HUMINT. Hewas a most welcome addition to Bryan Ranft's staff. He and I became not only close-working colleagues, we also became friends for life. Jamie McConnell was very much in the forefront of why I would be appointed to Washington DC in 1976, a career-changing event for me. I learned an enormous amount from Jamie about Russian sources and methods, and understanding their strategic thinking and how this devolved to their construction programs, operational deployments, and the use of naval power in pursuit of Soviet goals. He was immersed in Soviet military literature and thought. All this brushed off on me. I soaked up all that I could learn from someone who was the finest independent thinker, who did not and would not accept conventional wisdom as gospel. This great attribute was to pay dividends for the United States Navy, the UK, and their allies in the years from the early 1970s to the demise of the Soviet Union. In due course he and others, and I became one of them, would challenge various US intelligence assessments for both their accuracy and the data on which they were based. He had chosen to base himself at Greenwich rather than become attached to say the CIA Chief of Station's staff in the US Embassy in London, or work as a Defence Intelligence or Naval Intelligence analyst in the UK Ministry of Defence. He wanted intellectual independence and the freedom to move around those parts of the UK community that had a solid intellectual base to its work on the Soviet Union. This would include academia as well as the defense and intelligence community. He shared with me his seminal thinking on the direction in which the Soviet Union was moving in terms of the role and mission, and the detailed tactical deployment, of their key naval nuclear deterrent assets, their SSBNs, the equivalent in the early 1970s to the UK–US Polaris submarines. He began to postulate what was to become an incredibly accurate rendition of Soviet naval strategic thinking, embodied in what he termed a "Withholding Strategy," that Soviet SSBNs were the fallback second-strike nuclear assets after initial nuclear Armageddon commenced, and that the Soviet would seek to protect them and keep them sacrosanct in what he called "bastions." The latter were going to be under the Arctic ice cap, with the Soviets seeking locations near polynyas, or thin ice covers above the Arctic Ocean from which submarine-launched nuclear ballistic missiles could be launched as a second strike against the United States and its allies. This would entail the Soviets ice hardening their submarines and using the Arctic as the key bastion, others being defined as those sea areas within a defendable perimeter in the northern Norwegian Sea and the Barents Sea. These bastions would be fully protected by multiple tactical assets. This represented not just new and innovative thinking and assessment, it challenged conventional reports, analyses, and most all US National Intelligence Assessments (NIEs). The difference lay in the delta between strictly conventional intelligence sources and methods, the analytical product derived from these, and the McConnell approach that married these data sources with Soviet open sources. The latter was not easily available to Western sources and was more often than not obtained by surreptitious means. They were not often available for public use in the Soviet Union and although not classified as such was nonetheless restricted in distribution. Added to these more discreet Soviet open sources were the technical papers that Soviet scientists and engineers published within their specialist communities, again not classified but nonetheless with restrictive access. McConnell used these sources in spades and to great analytical effect. They were highly reliable and if read beside the highly classified UK–US intelligence sources new view could emerge of Soviet intentions. I immersed myself in his output, while realizing that we were all poor relations insofar as we could at best speak a few paltry words of Russian. McConnell was in a league of his own and the UK benefited not just from his time at Greenwich but as a result key British personnel became familiar with his methodology and product, learning greatly from him over the ensuing decades.

The Honorable Professor Alastair Buchan

I recall well in the early 1970s being notified that I had been selected together with one Royal Marine officer, two Army officers, and two Royal Air Force officers to attend a specially tailored course at Oxford University that was designed and led by the Honorable Professor Alastair Buchan (September 1918–February 1976, son of the famous author John Buchan and a former Governor General of Canada), the Montague Burton Professor of International Relations at Oxford. Prior to Oxford he had been Director of the International Institute of Strategic Studies and Commandant of the Imperial Defense College. He had fought in World War II in the Canadian Army. The course was demanding and an inspiration. I was the only one to have a full career in intelligence, but the relationships that I built were enduring, and what I learned from Alastair Buchan and my other mentors in the 1960s, I have, very subconsciously and subliminally, used in writing this book.

David Kahn

Through my intelligence and academic associations I was very familiar with the American, David Kahn (born 1930) author of *The Codebreakers—The Story of Secret Writing*, a very fine description and analysis of the history of cryptography from ancient Egypt through to the time of publication in 1967. I had studied David Kahn's work during my doctoral research, so when he came to St. Antony's College, Oxford as a research scholar, I planned to meet with him. David Kahn was awarded an Oxford DPhil in 1974 under the supervision of the Regius Professor of Modern History, Hugh Trevor-Roper, on modern German history. I was naturally keen to make his personal acquaintance. I visited him at Oxford during my many visits to the other Oxford luminaries mentioned earlier. I was intrigued by some of the difficulties that he experienced in publishing his book, with the US NSA wanting his publisher to redact various parts, even though he had used open sources. I gained much insight into his cryptologic research and how he had managed to amass such a monumental and magnificent data set. I regard David Kahn highly and his work has in my opinion been unsurpassed. He later in life donated all his key research papers and personal documents to the NSA archives. From the earlier differences with the US government David Kahn became a benefactor and much respected historian of the cryptologic arts and sciences that the NSA community embraced as one of their own.

Peter Jay

Peter Jay (1937–), had been commissioned in the Royal Navy, had also worked as a civil servant in the Treasury, and then moved to journalism, becoming for ten years the economics editor of the *Times*. Peter Jay was clearly intellectually gifted, having gained a "First" in PPE at Christ Church, Oxford, where he was also President of the Oxford Union. Peter Jay was the son of Douglas Jay (later Baron Jay), a Labour Party politician. He was a most capable and popular lecturer. He knew his subject extremely well and expounded with great clarity and humor. He answered questions on the British and world economies with consummate skill. I thought no more of this until one day I was summoned to the Admiral President's office. Rear Admiral "Teddy" Ellis was a delightful man, in his last post in the service before retirement. I knew his son well, who was also a Royal Navy officer close in seniority to myself. The admiral said he wanted me to do him a favor. I was intrigued naturally. He said that he could not order me to do what he was going to request, but clearly hoped that I would concur. He said that he was aware that I knew PeterJay through his visits to lecture and, here was the rub, he was the son-in-law of James Callaghan. The admiral explained that Peter Jay planned to sail this boat across the Atlantic to the United States. This was a time when there was no global positioning technology (GPS), and sail boats did not have Decca navigators or LORAN, a system that permitted ships to electronically plot their positions using radio bearings if they were in range of the LORAN transmitters. Peter Jay had let the Admiral President know that he very much wanted instruction on how to do astro-navigation and could he help find the right person to teach him. As it turned out, I was the only navigation instructor then on the college staff. Would I instruct him? "Yes, Sir, delighted to do so," rolled off my tongue. The admiral was delighted, and I left his office with a few extra points to my credit. I dutifully obeyed and to be very frank I thoroughly enjoyed the interaction. Peter Jay was exceptionally bright and I taught him the necessary skills to help him navigate safely across the Atlantic. Little did I realize that I was training the future Ambassador to the United States and that his father-in-law would become Prime Minister. In Washington DC a few years later, at the British Embassy, this would cause me a modicum ofdifficulty and explanation to my superiors, that is my relationship with the new Ambassador, who succeeded a distinguished and much-loved career diplomat, Sir Peter Ramsbotham (Ambassador 1974–1977), who was also very highly respected by the Americans and was a favorite of all the Embassy staff. On becoming Prime Minister in 1979 Margaret Thatcher was quick to ensure Peter Jay's departure from the British Embassy in Washington, replacing him with another career diplomat, Sir Nicholas Henderson.

Admiral Sir Nicholas Hunt and Admiral Sir James Eberle

Two senior Royal Navy officers during these years at sea were to have an abiding impact on my career and thinking. I had considerable respect for their leadership skills and their fine intellects. Both would in due course become four-star admirals and knighted for their services. The first was my captain in HMS *Intrepid*, Captain Nicholas Hunt (1930–2013; Commander-in-Chief Fleet, and Allied Commanderin- Chief Channel and Eastern Atlantic, 1985–1987), father of the young boy that I knew at this time who became the British Minister of Health and then Foreign Secretary until his resignation in 2019, Jeremy Hunt, MP (born 1966). While I was serving with Captain Hunt in HMS *Intrepid*, Rear Admiral James Eberle, a World War II veteran, was the Flag Officer Carriers and Amphibious Ships (1927–2018; Commander-in-Chief Fleet, 1979–1981; Commander-in-Chief Naval Home Command, 1981–1982; in retirement Director of the Royal Institute for International Affairs, 1984–1990). Both these officers influenced my thinking as well as my leadership skills, and I would remain in touch with both for the rest of my naval career and, in the case of Admiral Hunt, after I returned to the United States permanently in 1983. They were thinkers and both nurtured my own naval and strategic thinking. I owe them both a debt of gratitude for taking an interest in my career development. They set a wonderful example.

Daniel Patrick O'Connell

1973 was the 100th anniversary of the Royal Naval College, Greenwich (RNC Greenwich closed in 1998 when British higher military education was consolidated or all services in one location at a Joint Services Command and Staff College in Watchfield, Oxfordshire). Today this historic site is managed by the Greenwich Foundation for the Old Royal Naval College. I was privileged to be on the staff during this celebratory year, culminating in visit and dinner with Queen Elizabeth and other senior signatories. One key symposium-cum-conference that we held was I believe the first ever major gathering relating to the "Law of the Sea." As the junior member of the staff, at least by age, I was directed by the Admiral President to run all the logistics for the conference. The good news was that this allowed me interface with all the guest speakers and conferees, and of these one stood out aboveall others, and he became the single most important contributor, giving a series of outstanding addresses. This was Professor Daniel Patrick O'Connell (1924–1979), a New Zealander, born in Auckland, who was the Chichele Professor of Public International Law at Oxford, from 1972 until he died in 1979 in Oxford, and the Author of what I regard as still the major works on the law of the sea: *The Influence of Law on Sea Power* and *The International Law of the Sea* (published posthumously).3 The latter is a definitive work. Through O'Connell's seminal work and the publication of the Conference Records there was much impetus given through British government and naval channels to what became the United Nation as Convention on the Law of the Sea (UNCLOS for short), signed on December 10, 1982 by 157 signatory nations, with an effective date of November 16, 1994. Because of my logistics tasking I interacted with Professor O'Connell and he became very interested in our joint ideas on the intersection of intelligence with the law of the sea as he envisaged it in preserving international order, not simply on the high seas per se, but in the wider ramifications for international peace and order. I made several subsequent visits to Oxford to develop these ideas. My visits to Professor O'Connell also enabled me to renew the close associations developed with both Professor Buchan and Professor Trevor-Roper. It was an illuminating intellectual experience to see the coalescence of law, intelligence, and recent modern history coupled to their prognoses for the Cold War and dealing with the Soviet Union and its Warsaw pact allies. My involvement in the law of the sea through Professor O'Connell encouraged me to take a much wider and more detailed look at legal issues that much later would stand me in good stead when addressing international terrorism and the role of the sea, gun running, human trafficking, the international trade in dugs via the oceans of the world, and illegal weapons shipment. Today Chinese encroachments in the South China Sea and a Ruling by the International Court of Arbitration in The Hague against China continue my focus on not just the intelligence implications but the intertwined legal aspects. I became so involved intellectually in the law of the sea aspects that on July 29, 1975, while I was at sea in one of my next appointments after Greenwich, I was admitted to Lincoln's Inn, one of the four Inns of Court, to become in due course a British barrister.

Admiral Sir Herbert Richmond

The Greenwich academic staff had a private dining club that was only open to established academics in the key domains of naval strategy, plans, intelligence, and operations, and the whole panoply of current international relations and politics that underscored all the above. It was a select few and I was privileged to join the "Herbert Richmond Dining Club," named after Admiral Sir Herbert Richmond (1871–1946) who led, with others, the founding of *The Naval Review* in October 1912 with the following goal, "To promote the advancement and spreading within the Service (the Royal Navy) of knowledge relevant to the higher aspects of the Naval Profession." *The Naval Review* to this day is a vital source of high-quality thinking and discourse on all matters relevant to maritime strategy and operations and the myriad associated political–economic–social–diplomatic and historical factors. Richmond was not just a highly successful sea-going commander he was a distinguished intellectual, becoming after his retirement as a four-star admiral the Vere Harmsworth Professor of Imperial and Naval History from 1934–1936 and the Master of Downing College, Cambridge University from 1934–1946. He has been described as "perhaps the most brilliant naval officer of his generation," and as a first-class naval historian he was called the "British Mahan." He was successively in charge of the Senior Officers Course and then the Admiral President of the Royal Naval College, Greenwich 1920–1922. After retirement from the Royal Navy he had the foresight very early on to see the impact of the emerging Japanese threat and what the British government should do to counteract what he saw would become Japanese expansionism.

Vice Admiral Sir Roy "Gus" Halliday

When I served in Washington DC in the mid-1970s my reporting chain would be via Op-96 in the Office of the Chief of Naval Operations in the Pentagon to the British Naval Attaché, Rear Admiral Roy "Gus" Halliday (1923–2007). Admiral Halliday was a distinguished World War II veteran who won the Distinguished Service Cross (DSC) flying from HMS *Illustrious* and HMS *Victorious* against the Japanese from the British Pacific Fleet. He had been shot down and was rescued by HMS *Whelp*, whose First Lieutenant was Lieutenant Prince Philip of Greece, who lent Halliday a spare uniform and later the two of them celebrated on a "run ashore" in Fremantle. Halliday was back on-board HMS *Victorious* in time to take part in the raids on the airfields on the Sakishima Islands in March to May1945. He was awarded the DSC for his courageous efforts and he also received a "Mention in Dispatches" for his flying during Operation *Meridian*. After the Japanese surrender he learned that his cabin-mate, Ken Burrenston, had been shot down over Palembang, captured by the Japanese and then beheaded at the notorious Changi prisoner-of-war camp two days after the Japanese surrender, a heinous war crime. After a distinguished post-war career he was appointed Head of Naval Intelligence in 1973 (the DNI position had been abolished as part of the 1967 centralization initiated by Minister of Defence Denis Healey) as a Commodore, from which post he was promoted to Rear Admiral in 1975 and appointed Naval Attaché and Commander of the British Navy Staff in Washington DC. In 1978 now Vice Admiral Halliday became the Deputy Chief of the Defence Staff (Intelligence),. And on retirement from the Royal Navy in 1981 he was made the Director-General Intelligence at the Ministry of

Defence from 1981–1984. I was privileged to both work for Admiral Halliday in his various roles and appointments, and he became a significant champion of my interests and career development during and after my tour in Washington DC.

Admiral Carlisle "Carl" Trost

My American naval report in Washington DC in the mid-1970s was Rear Admiral Carlisle Trost, Op-96 (born April 24, 1930). He has always been known as Carl. From Illinois, Admiral Trost graduated first in the US Naval Academy class of 1953. He became a submariner and had an extraordinarily successful career; illustrious would be a much better description. In May 1986 he was nominated by President Ronald Reagan to succeed Admiral James Watkins as Chief of Naval Operations (CNO). Admiral Trost served as CNO from July 1986 to June 1990. I was therefore unbelievably fortunate to have as my US Naval direct report the officer would in due course become the CNO. Between Admiral Halliday and Admiral Trost who could ever expect to have such fine leaders with such distinguished careers both behind and ahead of them.

Vice Admiral Samuel L. Gravely Jr.

My finale during my appointment in Washington DC in the mid-1970s was actual sea time, in the nuclear-powered cruiser USS *Bainbridge* (CGN 25) in Third Fleet, US Pacific Fleet. I deployed for Exercise Varsity Sprint in the Pacific, sailing from San Diego. This was an enormous eye opener for me on just how prodigious the capabilities of the US Navy were. *Bainbridge* had recently fitted the Naval Tactical Data System (NTDS), by far the most advanced system of its kind in the world. I gained enormous hands-on experience on board *Bainbridge*. The Commander of the Third Fleet, Vice Admiral Samuel L. Gravely Jr. (1922–2004) was a remarkable and truly wonderful person and leader. I got to know him well during my time on *Bainbridge*. He was the first African American to serve aboard a fighting ship as an officer, the first to command a US Navy ship, the first to become a flag officer, and the first to command a numbered fleet, a hugely remarkable achievement for his generation. He and I interacted on many subjects, not least naturally the ongoing Sea War '85 project, Soviet intelligence matters, and comparisons and contrasts between the US Navy and the Royal Navy. He invited me to stand with him regularly on *Bainbridge*'s bridge wings as we conducted various evolutions. During Varsity Sprint *Bainbridge* demonstrated just how powerful a tool the NTDS was when coupled to the Terrier missile system. I transferred by helicopter to several other ships for short visits, including the battle group's aircraft carriers. It was a happy time, a great learning experience, and I hope that in my own small ways I contributed. I stayed in touch with Admiral Gravely after I returned to the UK, corresponding by private letter. He retired in 1980, and I was most upset when my schedule back in London would not permit me to attend his retirement ceremony at the Defense Communications Agency, where he was director. I regard him to this day as one of the finest people that I have been privileged to know.

USS *Bainbridge* (CGN 25). (Wikimedia Commons, US Navy)

Vice Admiral Samuel Gravely, United
States Navy. (Arlington Cemetery)

GLOSSARY OF TERMS

ACINT Acoustic Intelligence

AIS Automatic Identification System

ASIO Australia Security and Intelligence Organization

ASIS Australia Secret Intelligence Service

C The initial designating the Director of the British Secret Intelligence Service (The first Director of SIS was Captain Sir Mansfield Cumming, Royal Navy, who signed his documents with just the letter "C")

CIA Central Intelligence Agency

CinCPac Commander-in-Chief US Pacific Command

CinCPacFleet Commander-in-Chief US Pacific Fleet

CinCUSNavEur Commander-in-Chief US Naval Forces Europe

CJCS Chairman of the Joint Chiefs of Staff

CNO Chief of Naval Operations

CNA Center for Naval Analyses

COMINT Communications Intelligence

COMSUBPAC Commander Submarine Forces US Pacific Fleet

CONOPS Concepts of Operation

CSE Communications Security Establishment

DARPA Defense Advanced Research Projects Agency

DIA Defense Intelligence Agency

DIS Defence Intelligence Staff (later DI—Defence Intelligence)

DNA Deoxyribonucleic Acid

DNI Director of Naval Intelligence (UK and US) and Director of National Intelligence (US)

DOE Department of Energy (US)

ELECTRO-OPINT Electro-Optical Intelligence

ELINT Electronic Intelligence

FBE Fleet Battle Experiment

FBI Federal Bureau of Investigation

FEBA Forward Edge of the Battle Area

FISC Foreign Intelligence Surveillance Court

FSB Federal Security Service (Russia)

GC&CS Government Code and Cypher School

GCHQ Government Communications Headquarters

GCSB New Zealand Government Communications Security Bureau

GEOINT Geospatial Intelligence

GRU Intelligence Directorate of the General Staff of the Armed Forces of the former Soviet Union and currently of the Russian Federation

HASC House Armed Services Committee

HPSCI House Permanent Select Committee on Intelligence

IAEA International Atomic Energy Authority

IMINT Imagery Intelligence

IOC Initial Operational Capability

ISIS Islamic State in Iraq and Syria

I&W Indicators and Warning

JIC Joint Intelligence Committee

KGB The Committee for State Security was the main security agency of the Soviet Union from March 1954 until December 1991

LASINT Laser Intelligence

LOE Limited Objective Experiment

MAD Mutual Assured Destruction

MAD Magnetic Anomaly Detector

MASINT Measurement and Signature Intelligence

MI5 British Security Service

MI6 British Secret Intelligence Service (SIS)

NAB New Zealand National Assessment Bureau

NATO North Atlantic Treaty Organization

NCSC National Cyber Security Center

NCTC National Counterterrorism Center

NGA National Geospatial Agency

NID Naval Intelligence Department

NRO National Reconnaissance Office

NSA National Security Agency

NSC National Security Council (UK and US)

NUCINT Nuclear Intelligence

NZSIS New Zealand Secret Intelligence Service

ONI Office of Naval Intelligence

PFIAB President's Foreign Intelligence Advisory Board

RADINT Radar Intelligence

RCMP Royal Canadian Mounted Police

RDA R&D Associates

RF/EMPINT Radio Frequency and Electromagnetic Pulse Intelligence

RINT Radiation Intelligence

SEAL US Navy Sea Air Land Special Force Operator

SIGINT Signals Intelligence

SOSUS Sound Surveillance System

SSBN Nuclear-powered ballistic missile Submarine

SSGN Nuclear-powered guided missile Submarine

SSK Non-nuclear-powered diesel or air independent propulsion submarine

SSN Nuclear Powered attack Submarine

TTPs Tactics Techniques and Procedures

UAV Unmanned Aerial Vehicle

UCAV Unmanned Combat Aerial Vehicle

UNCLOS United Nations Convention on the Law of the Sea

UNO United Nations Organization

UUV Unmanned Underwater Vehicle

WMD Weapon(s) of Mass Destruction

BIBLIOGRAPHY

Abshagen, K. H. *Canaris*. Translated by A. H. Brodrick. London: Hutchinson, 1956.

Admiralty British. Fuhrer Conference on Naval Affairs. Admiralty 1947. London: Her Majesty's Stationery Office.

Aid, M. *Secret Sentry: The Untold History of the National Security Agency*. New York: Bloomsbury, 2009.

Aldrich, R. J. Editor. *British Intelligence, Strategy, and the Cold War. 1945–1951*. London: Routledge, 1992.

Aldrich, R. J. Editor. *Espionage, Security, and Intelligence in Britain, 1945–1970*. Manchester: Manchester University Press, 1998.

Aldrich R. J. *Intelligence and the war against Japan: Britain, America and the Politics of Secret Service*. Cambridge: Cambridge University Press, 1999.

Aldrich R. J. *The Hidden Hand: Britain, America, and Cold War Secret Intelligence*. London: John Murray, 2001.

Aldrich R. J., G. Rawnsley and M. Y. Rawnsley, eds. *The Clandestine Cold War in Asia 1945–1965*. London: Frank Cass, 1999.

Aldrich R. J. and M. F Hopkins, eds. *Intelligence, Defense, and Diplomacy: British Policy in the Post War World*. London: Frank Cass, 1994.

Aldrich, Richard J. *GCHQ The Uncensored Story of Britain's Most Secret Intelligence Agency*. London: Harper Press, 2010.

Alsop, Stewart and Braden, Thomas. *Sub Rosa. The OSS and American Espionage*. New York: Reynal and Hitchcock, 1946.

Andrew, C. M. *Secret Service: The Making of the British Intelligence Community.* London: Heinemann, 1985.

Andrew, C. M. *For the President's Eyes Only: Secret Intelligence and the American Presidency from Washington to Bush.* London: Harper Collins, 1995.

Andrew, C. M. *Defense of the Realm. The Official History of the Security Service.* London: Allen Lane, 2009.

Andrew, C. M. and D. Dilks, eds. *The Missing Dimension: Governments and Intelligence Communities in the Twentieth Century.* London: Macmillan, 1982.

Andrew, C. M. and O. Gordievsky. *KGB: The Inside Story.* London: Hodder and Stoughton, 1990.

Andrew, C. M. and V. Mitrokhin. *The Sword and the Shield: The Mitrokhin Archive and the Secret History of the KGB.* New York: Basic Books, 1999.

Arnold, H. *Global Mission. Chief of the Army Air Forces 1938–1946.* New York: Harper, 1949.

Assman, K. *Deutsche Seestrategie in Zwei Welkriegen.* Vowinckel. Heidelberg: Heidelberg Press, 1959.

Aston, Sir George. *Secret Service.* London: Faber and Faber, 1939.

Bamford, J. *The Puzzle Palace: America's National Security Agency and its Special Relationship with GCHQ.* London: Sidgwick and Jackson, 1983.

Bamford, J. *Body of Secrets: How NSA and Britain's GCHQ Eavesdrop on the World.* New York: Doubleday, 2001.

Bamford, J. *The Shadow Factory: The Ultra-Secret NSA from 9/11 to Eavesdropping on America.* New York: Doubleday, 2008.

Barrass, Gordon S. *The Great Cold War: A Journey Through the Hall of Mirrors.* Stanford, California: Stanford University, 2009.

Barry and Creasy. *Attacks on the Tirpitz by Midget Submarines.* September 1943. *London Gazette,* July 3, 1947.

Beardon, Milton, and James Risen. *The Main Enemy: The Inside Story of the CIA's Final Showdown with the KGB.* London: Penguin Random House, 2003.

Bedell Smith, W. *Eisenhower's Six Great Decisions*. London: Longmans, 1956.

Bennett, G. *Churchill's Man of Mystery: Desmond Morton and the World of Intelligence*. London: Routledge, 2007.

Bennett, R. *Ultra in the West: The Normandy Campaign of 1944–1945*. London: Hutchinson, 1979.

Blackburn, D. and W. Caddell. *Secret Service in South Africa*. London: Cassell and Company London, 1911.

Belot, R. *The Struggle for the Mediterranean 1939–1945*. Oxford: Oxford University Press, 1951.

Benjamin, R. *Five Lives in One. An Insider's View of the Defence and Intelligence World*. Tunbridge Wells: Parapress, 1996.

Benson, R. L. and R. Warner. *Venona: Soviet Espionage and the American Response, 1939–1957. Menlo Park*. California: Aegean Park Press, 1997.

Bilton, M. and P. Kosminksy. *Speaking Out: Untold Stories from the Falklands War*. Grafton: Grafton, 1987.

Booth, K. *Navies and Foreign Policy*. New York: Croom Helm, 1977.

Borovik, Genrikh. *The Philby Files: The Secret Life of Master Spy Kim Philby—KGB Archives Revealed*. London: Little Brown, 1994.

Brodie, Bernard. *Strategy in the Missile Age*. Princeton: Princeton University Press, 1959.

Brodie, Bernard. *The Future of Deterrence in U.S. Strategy*. California: University of California Press, 1968.

Brodie, Bernard. *War and Politics*. London: Macmillan, 1973.

Buchan, Alastair. *War in Modern Society*. Oxford: Oxford University, 1966

Buchan, Alastair. *The End of the Postwar Era: A New Balance of World Power*. Oxford: Oxford University, 1974.

Cable, James. *Britain's Naval Future*. Annapolis, Maryland: US Naval Institute Press, 1983.

Calvocoressi, P. *Top Secret Ultra*. London: Cassell and Company London, 1980.

Carrington, Lord. *Reflect on Things Past. The Memoirs of Lord Carrington*. London: Collins, 1988.

Carl, Leo D. *The International Dictionary of Intelligence*. Virginia: McLean, 1990.

Carter, Miranda. *Anthony Blunt: His Lives*. London: Farrar, Straus, & Giroux, 2001.

Cater, D. *The Fourth Branch of Government*. Boston: Houghton Mifflin, 1959.

Cavendish, A. *Inside Intelligence*. London: Harper Collins, 1990.

Cherkashin, A. *Spy Handler. Memoirs of a KGB Officer*. New York: Basic Books, 2005.

China. The State Council Information Office of the People's Republic of China: In the New Era. July 2019. This is an open source Chinese government official publication and policy statement.

Clayton, A. *The Enemy is Listening: The Story of the Y Service*. London: Hutchinson, 1980.

Cockburn, Andrew and Leslie: *Dangerous Liaison. The Inside Story of the US-Israeli Covert Relationship*. Place: Harper Collins, 1991.

Cocker, M. P. *Royal Navy Submarines 1901–1982*. London: Frederick Warre Publications, 1982.

Cole, D. J. *Geoffrey Prime: The Imperfect Spy*. London: Robert Hale, 1998.

Colvin, I. *Chief of Intelligence*. London: Gollanz, 1951.

Colomb J. C. R. "Naval Intelligence and the Protection of Shipping in War," *RUSI Journal*, vol. 25 (1882): 553–590.

Compton-Hall, Richard. *Subs versus Subs. The Tactical Technology of Underwater Warfare*. London: David and Charles Publishers, 1988.

Copeland, B. J. *Colossus: The Secrets of Bletchley Park's Code-Breaking Computers*. Oxford: Oxford University Press, 2006.

Corera, Gordon. *MI6: Life and Death in the British Secret Service*. London: Harper Collins, 2012.

Dalein, D. J. *Soviet Espionage*. Oxford: Oxford University Press, 1955.

Deacon, R. *A History of the British Secret Service*. London: Muller, 1969.

De Silva, P. *Sub Rosa: The CIA and the Use of Intelligence*. New York: Times Books, 1978.

Dismukes, B. and McConnell J. *Soviet Naval Diplomacy*. New York: Pergamon Press, 1979.

Driberg, T. *Guy Burgess*. London: Weidenfeld and Nicholson, 1956.

Dulles, Allen. *The Craft of Intelligence*. New York: Harper and Row, 1963.

Dumbrell, J. *Special Relationship: Anglo-American Relations from the Cold War to Iraq*. London: Palgrave, 2006.

Earley, Peter. *Confessions of a Spy: The Real Story of Aldrich Ames*. New York: Putnam & Son, 1997.

Elliott, G. and H. Shukman. *Secret Classrooms. An untold story of the Cold War*. London: St. Ermin's Press, 2002.

Everitt, Nicholas. *British Secret Service during the Great War*. London: Hutchinson, 1920.

Ewing, A. W. *The Man of Room 40. The Life of Sir Alfred Ewing*. London: Hutchinson, 1939.

Fahey, J. A. *Licensed to Spy*. Annapolis, Maryland: US Naval Institute Press, 2002.

Falconer, D. *First into Action: A Dramatic Personal Account of Life in the SBS*. London: Little Brown, 2001.

Fanell, James. "China's Worldwide Military Expansion." Testimony and Statement for the Record. US House of Representatives Permanent Select Committee on Intelligence. Hearing, May 15, 2018. Rayburn Building, Washington DC.

Fishman, Charles. *One Giant Leap. The Impossible Mission that Flew us to the Moon*. New York: Simon and Schuster, 2019.

Fitzgerald, P. and M. Leopold. *Strangers on the Line: A Secret History of Phone-Tapping*. London: Bodley Head, 1987.

Freedman, Sir Lawrence. *Strategy*. Oxford: Oxford University Press, 2013.

Freedman, Sir Lawrence. *Official History of the Falklands Campaign. Volumes 1 and 2*. London: Routledge, 2005.

Freedman, Sir Lawrence and Gamba-Stonehouse, V. *Signals of War: The Falklands Conflict of 1982*. Princeton: Princeton University Press, 1991.

Freedman, Sir Lawrence. *A Choice of Enemies: America Confronts the Middle East*. Oxford: Oxford University Press, 2008.

Friedman, Norman. *Submarine Design and Development. Conway Maritime Press*. London: Conway, 1984.

Friedman, Norman. *The Fifty-Year Conflict: Conflict and Strategy in the Cold War*. Annapolis. Maryland: Naval Institute Press, 2007.

Foote, A. *Handbook for Spies*. London: Museum Press, 1949.

Foot, M. R. D. *SOE in France*. London: Her Majesty's Stationery Office, 1964.

Friedman, W. F. and C. J. Mendelsohn. *The Zimmermann Telegram of January 16, 1917 and its cryptographic background*. US War department, Office of the Chief Signal Officer. Washington DC: US Government Printing Office, 1938.

Frost, M. *Spyworld: Inside the Canadian and American Intelligence Establishments*. Toronto: Doubleday, 1994.

Fuchida, Mitsuo and Okumiya Masutake. Edited by Roger Pineau and Clarke Kawakami. *Midway, The Battle that Doomed Japan. The Japanese Navy's Story*. Annapolis, Maryland: Blue Jacket, 1955.

Gaddis, John Lewis. *The Cold War*. London: 2007.

Ganguly, Sumit and Chris Mason. "An Unnatural Partnership? The Future of US-India Strategic Cooperation. Strategic Studies Institute." US Army War College. May 2019.

Gates, Robert. *From the Shadows: The Ultimate Insider's Story of Five Presidents and How They Won the Cold War*. New York: Simon & Schuster, 2006.

George, James, ed. *The Soviet and Other Communist Navies.* Annapolis, Maryland: US Naval Institute Press, 1986.

Godfrey, Vice Admiral John. *Naval Memoirs.* London: National Maritime Museum Greenwich, 1965.

Goodman, M. S. *Spying on the Nuclear Bear: Anglo-American Intelligence and the Soviet Bomb.* Stanford, California: Stanford University Press, 2007.

Gordievsky, Oleg. *Next Stop Execution: The Autobiography of Oleg Gordievsky.* London: Whole Story, 1995.

Graham, G. S. *The Politics of Naval Supremacy.* Cambridge: Cambridge University Press, 1965.

Grant, R. M. *U-Boat Intelligence, 1914–1918.* Connecticut: Hamden, 1969.

Grayson, W. C. *Chicksands. A Millennium History.* London: Shefford Press, 1992.

Grimes, Sandra, and Jeanne Vertefeuille. *Circle of Treason: A CIA Account of Traitor Aldrich Ames and the Men He Betrayed.* Annapolis, Maryland: Naval Institute Press, 2012.

Halevy, Efraim. *Man in the Shadows. Inside the Middle East Crisis with a man who led the Mossad.* London: Weidenfeld and Nicholson, 2006.

Harper, Stephen. *Capturing Enigma. How HMS Petard Seized the German Naval Codes.* London: The History Press, 2008.

Hastings, Max with Simon Jenkins. *The Battle for the Falklands.* New York: W.W. Norton and Company, 1983.

Healey, D. *The Time of My Life.* London: Michael Joseph, 1989.

Bibliography • 231

Helms, Richard. *A Look over My Shoulder: A Life in the Central Intelligence Agency.* New York: Random House, 2003.

Hendrick, B. J. *The Life and Letters of Walter H. Page.* Garden City, New York: Yale University Press, 1922.

Herman, M. *Intelligence Power in Peace and War.* Cambridge: Cambridge University Press, 1992.

Herman, M. *Intelligence Services in the Information Age.* London: Cassell and Company London, 2001.

Higham, R. *Armed Forces in Peacetime. Britain 1918–1940. A Case Study*. London: Foulis Press, 1963.

Hill, Rear Admiral J. R. *Anti-Submarine Warfare*. United States Naval Institute Press. Annapolis, Maryland. 1985.

Hill, Rear Admiral J. R., ed. *Oxford Illustrated History of the Royal Navy*. Oxford: Oxford University Press, 1995.

Hill, Rear Admiral J. R. *Lewin of Greenwich. The Authorized Biography of Admiral of the Fleet Lord Lewin*. London: Cassell and Company London, 2000.

Hillsman, Roger. *Strategic Intelligence and National Decisions*. Cambridge: Cambridge University Press, 1956.

Hinsley, F. H. *British Intelligence in the Second World War*. London: Her Majesty's Stationery Office, 1979–1990.

Hinsley, F. H. *Hitler's Strategy*. Cambridge: Cambridge University Press, 1951.

Hinsley, F. H. and A. Stripp, eds. *Code-Breakers: The Inside Story of Bletchley Park*. Oxford: Oxford University Press, 1993.

Hoffman, David E. *The Billion Dollar Spy: A True Story of Cold War Espionage and Betrayal*. New York: Penguin Random House, 2015.

Hollander, Paul. *Political Will and Personal Belief: The Decline and Fall of Soviet Communism*. New Haven, Connecticut: Yale University, 1999.

Howard, Sir Michael. *Captain Professor: A Life in War and Peace*. New York: Continuum Press, 2006.

Howard, Sir Michael. *Liberation or Catastrophe: Reflections on the History of the 20th Century*. London: A and C Black, 2007.

Howe, Geoffrey. *Conflict of Loyalty*. London: Macmillan, 1994.

Hunt, Sir David. *A Don at War*. London: Harper Collins, 1966.

International Institute for Strategic Studies (IISS). *The Military Balance Collection*. London: IISS, 2020.

Ireland, Bernard. With Eric Grove. *War at Sea 1897–1997*. London: Harper Collins and Janes, 1997.

James, Admiral Sir William. "The Eyes of the Navy. Room 40." *Edinburgh University Journal*, no. 22 (Spring 1965): 50–54.

Janes Fighting Ships. London: Janes Publishing, 1960–2015.

Jeffery, Keith. *MI6: The History of the Secret Intelligence Service, 1909–1949*. London: Penguin Random House, 2010.

Jenkins, R. *Life at the Centre*. London: Macmillan, 1991.

Johnson, Adrian L., ed. *Wars in Peace*. London: Royal United Service Institution, 2014.

Johnson, T. R. *American Cryptology during the Cold War, 1945–1989*. Volumes 1–4. United States National Security Agency. Declassified in 2009.

Jones, Nate, ed. *Able Archer '83: The Secret History of the NATO Exercise that Almost Triggered Nuclear War*. New York: The New Press, 2016.

Jones, R. V. *Most Secret War*. London: Hamish Hamilton Limited, 1978.

Kagan, Neil and Stephen G. Hyslop. *The Secret History of World War 2*. Washington DC: National Geographic.

Kahn, David. *The Codebreakers*. London: Weidenfeld & Nicholson, 1966.

Kalugin, O. and F. Montaigne. *The First Directorate: My First 32 years in intelligence and espionage against the West—the ultimate memoirs of a Master Spy*. New York: St. Martin's Press, 1994.

Kendall, W. "The Functions of Intelligence." *World Politics*, no. 4, vol. 1 (July 1949): 542–552.

Kegan, John. *Intelligence in War*. New York: Vintage Books & Random House, 2002

Kendall, Bridget. *The Cold War: A New Oral History of Life Between East and West*. London: Penguin Books, 2018.

Kent, S. *Strategic Intelligence for American World Policy*. Oxford: Oxford University Press, 1949.

Korbel, J. *The Communist Subversion of Czechoslovakia, 1938–1948*. Oxford: Oxford University Press, 1959.

Kot, S. *Conversations with the Kremlin and Dispatches from Russia*. Oxford: Oxford University Press, 1963.

Krupakar, Jayanna. "Chinese Naval Base in the Indian Ocean. Signs of a Maritime Grand Strategy." *Strategic Analysis*, no. 3, vol. 41 (2017): 207–222

Lamphere, R. J. and T. Shachtman. *The FBI-KGB war: A Special Agent's Story*. London: W. H. Allen, 1986.

Lewis, Norman. *The Honoured Society*. London: Collins, 1964

Liddell-Hart, Sir B. H. *Strategy—the Indirect Approach*. London: Faber & Faber, 1954.

Liddell-Hart, Sir B. H. *The Other Side of the Hill*. London: Cassell, 1951.

Liddell-Hart, Sir B. H. *Memoirs in Two Volumes*. London: Cassell, 1965.

Liddell-Hart, Sir B. H. *The Real War, 1914–1918*. Boston: Little Brown & Company, 1930.

Lockhart, Sir Robert Bruce. *Memories of a British Agent*. London: Putnam, 1932.

Lockhart, Robin. *The Ace of Spies*. London: Hodder & Stoughton, 1967.

Lyubimov, Mikhail. *Notes of a Ne'er-Do-Well Rezident or Will-o'-the-Wisp*. Moscow: 1995.

Lyubimov, Mikhail. *Spies I Love and Hate*. Moscow: AST Olimp, 1997.

Macintyre, Ben. *The Spy and the Traitor*. London: Crown Publishing Group, 2018.

Marder, A. J. *From the Dreadnought to Scapa Flow*. 5 Volumes. Oxford: Oxford University Press, 1940.

Marder, A. J. *The Anatomy of British Sea Power*. New York: Alfred Knopf, 1940.

Martin, Sir Laurence. *Arms and Strategy*. London: Weidenfeld & Nicholson, 1973.

Mathams, R. H. *Sub-Rosa: Memoirs of an Australian Intelligence Analyst*. Sydney: Allen & Unwin, 1982.

McGehee, R. W. *Deadly Deceit: My 25 Years in the CIA*. New York: Sheridan Square, 1983.

McKay, Sinclair. *The Secret Life of Bletchley Park*. London: Aurum Press Limited, 2010.

McKay, Sinclair. *The Lost World of Bletchley Park*. London: Aurum Press Limited, 2013.

McKay, Sinclair. *The Secret Listeners*. London: Aurum Press Limited, 2013.

McKnight, D. *Australia's Spies and Their Secrets*. London: University College London Press, 1994.

McLachlan, Donald. *Room 39. Naval Intelligence in Action, 1939–1945*. London: Weidenfeld & Nicholson, 1968.

Mikesh, R. C. B-57: *Canberra at War*. London: Ian Allan, 1980.

Mitchell, M. and T. Mitchell. *The Spy Who Tried to Stop a War: Katharine Gun and the Secret Plot to Sanction the Iraq Invasion*. London: Polipoint Press, 2008.

Monat, P. *Spy in the US*. New York: Harper & Row, 1961.

Montagu, E. E. S. *The Man Who Never Was*. London: Evans Brothers, 1953.

Montgomery Hyde, H. *George Blake: Superspy*. London: Futura, 1987.

Moore, Charles. *Margaret Thatcher: The Authorized Biography. Volume 2. Everything She Wants*. London: Allen Lane, 2015.

Moorehead, A. *The Traitors*. London: Hamish Hamilton, 1952.

Morley, Jefferson. *The Ghost: The Secret Life of CIA Spymaster James Jesus Angleton*. London: St. Martin's Press, 2017.

Murphy, D. E., S. A. Kondrashev and G. Bailey. *Battleground Berlin: CIA vs. KGB in the Cold War*. New Haven: Yale University Press, 1997.

Nicolai, Colonel W. *The German Secret Service*. Translated by G. Renwick. Frankfurt am Main: Fischer, 2007.

Nott, J. *Here Today Gone Tomorrow: Recollections of an Errant Politician*. London: Politico's, 2002.

Oberdorfer, Don. *From the Cold War to a New Era: The United States and the Soviet Union, 1983–1991*. Baltimore, Maryland: John Hopkins University Press, 1998.

Orlov, Alexander. *Handbook of Intelligence and Guerrilla Warfare.* London: Cresset Press, 1963.

Packard, W. *A Century of Naval Intelligence.* Washington DC: Office of Naval Intelligence, 1996.

Parrish, T. *The Ultra Americans: The US Role in Breaking Nazi Codes.* New York: Stein and Day, 1986.

Parker, Philip, Editor. *The Cold War Spy Pocket Manual.* Oxford: Pool of London Press, 2015.

Paterson, M. *Voices of the Codebreakers: Personal Accounts of the Secret Heroes of World War Two.* Newton Abbot: David and Charles, 2007.

Pavlov, V. *Memoirs of a Spymaster: My Fifty Years in the KGB.* New York: Carroll and Graf., 1994.

Pawle, G. *The Secret War.* London: Harrap, 1972

Pearson, John. *The Life of Ian Fleming.* London: Jonathan Cape, 1966.

Petter, G. S. *The Future of American Secret Intelligence.* Washington DC: Hoover Press, 1946.

Petrov, Vladimir and Evdokia. *Empires of Fear.* London: Andre Deutsch, 1956.

Philby, Kim. *My Silent War.* New York: Grove Press, 1968.

Pincher, C. *Too Secret Too Long.* London: Sidgwick and Jackson, 1984.

Pincher, C. *Traitors: Labyrinths of Treason.* London: Sidgwick and Jackson, 1987.

Pincher, Chapman. *Treachery: Betrayals, Blunders, and Cover Ups: Six Decades of Espionage.* Edinburgh: Mainstream Publishing, 2012.

Polmar, Norman. *The Ships and Aircraft of the US Fleet.* Volumes. Annapolis, Maryland: United States Naval Institute Press, 1984.

Powers, T. *The Man who Kept the Secrets: Richard Helms and the CIA.* London: Weidenfeld and Nicholson, 1979.

Pratt, F. *Secret and Urgent. The Story of Codes and Ciphers.* London: Robert Hale, 1939.

Primakov, Yevgeny. *Russian Crossroads: Toward the New Millennium*. New Haven, Connecticut: Yale, 2004.

Prime, R. *Time of Trial: The Personal Story Behind the Cheltenham Spy Scandal*. London: Hodder & Stoughton, 1984.

Raeder, E. *Struggle for the Sea*. Translated by Edward Fitzgerald. London: Kimber, 1959.

Ramsay, Sir Bertram Home. "The Evacuation from Dunkirk, May–June 1940," *The London Gazette*, July 17, 1947.

Ramsay, Sir Bertram Home. "Assault Phases of the Normandy Landings, June 1944," *The London Gazette*, October 30, 1947.

Ranft, Bryan, ed. *Technical Change and British Naval Policy 1860–1939*. London: Hodder and Stoughton, 1977.

Ranelagh, J. *The Agency: The Rise and Decline of the CIA*. New York: Simon and Shuster, 1986.

Ranft, Bryan. "The Naval Defense of British Sea-Borne Trade, 1860–1905." D.Phil thesis, Balliol College, Oxford University, 1967.

Ransom, H. H. *Central Intelligence and the National Security*. Oxford: Oxford University Press, 1958.

Ratcliffe, P. *Eye of the Storm: Twenty-Five Years in Action with the SAS*. London: Michael O'Mara, 2000.

Rej, Abhijnan. "How India's Defense Policy Complicates US-India Military Cooperation." US Army War College. February 26, 2019. https://warroom.armywarcollege.edu/articles/indias-defense-policy-and-us/

Richelson, J. *A Century of Spies: Intelligence in the Twentieth Century*. Oxford: Oxford University Press, 1995.

Richelson, J. *The US Intelligence Community*. New York: Ballinger, 1989.

Richelson, J. *The Wizards of Langley: Inside the CIA's Directorate of Science and Technology*. Boulder, Colorado: Westview Press, 2001.

Richelson, J. and D. Ball. *Ties that Bind: Intelligence Cooperation Between the UKUSA Countries*. Boston: Allen and Unwin, 1985.

Report of the Security Commission, May 1983. Cmnd 8876. Her Majesty's Stationery Office, 1983

Report of the Security Commission, October 1986. Cmnd 9923. Her Majesty's Stationery Office, 1986.

Rintelen, Captain Franz Von. *The Dark Invader*. London: Peter Davis, 1933.

Roberts, Captain Jerry. *Lorenz. Breaking Hitler's Top Secret Code at Bletchley Park*. Cheltenham: The History Press, 2017.

Roskill, S. W. *The War at Sea. 1939–1945*. Three Volumes. London: Her Majesty's Stationery Office, 1954–1961.

Roskill, S. W. *Hankey, Man of Secrets*. London: Collins, 1969.

Rowan, R. W. *The Story of Secret Service*. London: Miles, 1938.

Ruge, F. *Sea Warfare 1939–1945. A German Viewpoint*. Translated by M. G. Saunders. London: Cassell, 1957.

Ryan, C. *The Longest Day, June 6, 1944*. New York: Simon & Schuster, 1960.

Sainsbury, A. B. *The Royal Navy Day by Day*. London: Ian Allen Publications, 1993.

Saran, Samir & Verma Richard Rahul. "Strategic Convergence: The United States and India as Major Defense Partners." Observer Research Foundation (ORF), June 25, 2019.

Scott, James. *The Attack on the Liberty. The Untold Story of Israel's Deadly 1967 Assault on a US Spy Ship*. New York: Simon & Schuster, 2009.

Schelling, W. R. *Strategy, Politics, and Defense Budgets*. New York: Columbia University Press, 1962.

Schull, J. *The Far Distant Ships. An Official Account of Canadian Naval Operations in the Second World War*. Ottawa: Ministry of National Defence, 1962.

Schurman, D. M. *The Education of a Navy: The Development of British Naval Strategic Thought, 1867–1914*. Oxford: Oxford University Press, 1966.

Sebag Montefiore, Simon. *Stalin: The Court of the Red Tsar*. London: Vintage, 2003.

Showell, Jak P. Mallmann. *German Naval Code Breakers*. London: Ian Allan Publishing, 2003.

Sides, Hampton. *On Desperate Ground. The Marines at the Reservoir. The Korean War's Greatest Battle*. New York: Doubleday, 2018.

Sillitoe, Sir Percy. "My Answer to Critics of MI5." *The Sunday Times*, November 22, 1953.

Singh, Zorawar Daulet. "Foreign Policy and Sea Power. India's Maritime Role." Center for Policy Research, Delhi. *Journal of Defense Studies*, no. 4, (2017).

Smith, B. F. *The Ultra-Magic Deals and the Most Secret Special Relationship 1940–1946*. Shrewsbury: Airlife Publishing, 1993.

Smith, B. F. *Sharing Secrets with Stalin: How the Allies Traded Intelligence, 1941–1945*. Kansas: University of Kansas Press, 1996.

Smith, M. *New Cloak. Old Dagger: How Britain's spies came in from the cold*. London: Victor Gollanz, 1996.

Smith, M. *Station X: The Code-Breakers of Bletchley Park*. London: Channel Four Books, 1998.

Smith, M. *The Emperor's Codes: Bletchley Park and the Breaking of Japan's Secret Ciphers*. London: Bantam, 2000.

Smith, M. *The Spying Game: A Secret History of British Espionage*. London: Politico's, 2003.

Smith, M. *Killer Elite: The Inside Story of America's Most Secret Operations Team*. New York: St. Martin's Press, 2007.

Smith, M. and R. Erskine, eds. *Action this Day: Bletchley Park from the breaking of the Enigma Code to the Birth of the Modern Computer*. London: Bantam, 2001.

Sontag, S. and Drew, C. *Blind Man's Bluff: The Untold Story of American Submarine Espionage*. New York: Public Affairs, 1998.

Stafford, D. *Spies Beneath Berlin*. Second Edition. London: John Murray, 2002.

Stein, H., ed. *American Civil-Military Decisions*. Birmingham, Alabama: University of Alabama Press, 1963.

Steinhauer, G. and Felsted, S. T. *The Kaiser's Master Spy*. London: John Lane, Bodley Head, 1930.

Strip, A. J. *Code Breakers in the Far East*. London: Frank Cass, 1989.

Strong, Major General Sir Kenneth. *Intelligence at the Top*. London: Cassell, 1968.

Sudoplatov, P. *Special Tasks: The Memoirs of an Unwanted Witness—a Soviet Spymaster*. London: Little Brown, 1994.

Sunday Express Magazine, London. *War in the Falklands: The Campaign in Pictures*. London: Weidenfeld & Nicholson Ltd, 1982.

Svendsen, A. *Intelligence Cooperation and the War on terror: Anglo-American Security Relations after 911*. London: Routledge, 2009.

Thakur, Arvind and Michael Padgett. "Time is Now to Advance US-India Defense Cooperation," *National Defense*, May 31, 2018.

Thatcher, M. *The Downing Street Years*. London: Harper Collins, 1993.

Thomas, R. *Espionage and Secrecy: The Official Secrets Act 1911–1989 of the United Kingdom*. London: Routledge, 1991.

Thompson, Julian. *No Picnic. 3 Commando Brigade in the South Atlantic 1982*. New York: Hippocrene Books, 1985.

Thompson, Tommy. "The Kremlinologist. Briefing Book Number 648." George Washington University, November 2018.

Thomson, Sir Basil. *The Story of Scotland Yard*. London: Grayson & Grayson, 1935.

Trento, Joseph J. *The Secret History of the CIA*. Roseville, California: Prima Publishing, 2001.

Tuchman, Barbara W. *The Zimmermann Telegram*. New York: Viking Press, 1958.

Toynbee, A., ed. *Survey of International Relations, 1939–1946*. Oxford: Oxford University Press,1952.

United States Department of Defense. "Preparedness, Partnerships, and Promoting a Networked Region." Indo-Pacific Strategy Report. Washington DC, June 1, 2019.

United States Department of Defense. Soviet Military Power. An annual publication from September 1981 to September 1990. This series may be obtained from the Superintendent of Documents, US Government Printing Office, Washington DC, 20402. This outstanding series, contains extensive unclassified detail of Soviet: Policies and Global Ambitions; Forces for Nuclear Attack; Strategic Defense and Space Operations; Forces for Theater Operations; Readiness, Mobility, and Sustainability; Research, Development, and Production; Political–Military and Regional Policies; The US response.

United States Department of State. "Intelligence: A Bibliography of its Functions, Methods, and Techniques." Part 1. December 1948. Part 2. April 1949.

Urban, M. *UK Eyes Alpha: The Inside Story of British Intelligence.* London: Faber and Faber, 1996.

Vickers, Philip. *A Clear Case of Genius. Room 40's Code-breaking Pioneer. Autobiography of Admiral Sir Reginald Hall.* Cheltenham: The History Press, 2017.

Vincent. J. *The Culture of Secrecy: Britain 1832–1988.* Oxford: Oxford University Press, 1998.

Waters, D. W. *A Study of the Philosophy and Conduct of Maritime War, 1815–1945.* Parts 1 and 2. Published privately. Copies are in the UK Ministry of Defence Library (Navy), and the National Maritime Museum, London.

Weiner, Tim, David Johnston and Neil A. Lewis. *Betrayal: The Story of Aldrich Ames, an American Spy.* London: Penguin Random House, 1996.

Wells, Anthony. "The 1967 June War: Soviet Naval Diplomacy and the Sixth Fleet—A Reappraisal." Center for Naval Analyses, Professional Paper 204, 1977, Department of the Navy.

Wells, Anthony. "NATO and US Carrier Deployment Policies." Center for Naval Analyses, February 1977, Department of the Navy.

Wells, Anthony. "Sea War '85 Scenario." With Captain John L. Underwood, United States Navy. *Center for Naval Analyses*, April 1977, Department of the Navy.

Wells, Anthony. "NATO and Carrier Deployment Policies: Formation of a new Standing Naval Strike Force in NATO." Center for Naval Analyses, April 1977, Department of the Navy.

Wells, Anthony. "The Application of Drag Reduction and Boundary Layer Control Technologies in an Experimental Program." Report for the Chief Naval Architect, Vickers Shipbuilding and Engineering Ltd, January 1986.

Wells, Anthony. "Preliminary Overview of Soviet Merchant Ships in SSBN Operations and Soviet Merchant Ships and Submarine Masking." SSBN Security Program, Department of the Navy, 1986, US Navy Contract N00016-85-C-0204.

Wells, Anthony. "SSBN Port Egress and the Non-Commercial Activities of the Soviet Merchant Fleet: Concepts of Operation and War Orders for Current and Future Anti-SSBN Operations." SSBN Security program, 1986, Department of the Navy, US Navy Contract N136400.

Wells, Anthony. "Overview Study of the Maritime Aspects of the Nuclear Balance in the European Theater." US Department of Energy Study for the European Conflict Analysis Project, October 1986, US Department of Energy.

Wells, Anthony. "The Soviet Navy in the Arctic and North Atlantic." *National Defense*, February 1986.

Wells, Anthony. "Soviet Submarine Prospects 1985–2000," *The Submarine Review*, January 1986.

Wells, Anthony. "A New Defense Strategy for Britain." *Proceedings of the United States Naval Institute*, March 1987.

Wells, Anthony. "Presence and Military Strategies of the USSR in the Arctic." Quebec Center for International Relations, Laval University Press, 1986.

Wells, Anthony. "Soviet Submarine Warfare Strategy Assessment and Future US Submarine and Anti- Submarine Warfare Technologies." Defense Advanced Research Projects Agency, March 1988, US Department of Defense.

Wells, Anthony. "Operational Factors Associated with the Software Nuclear Analysis for the UGM-109A Tomahawk Submarine-launched Land Attack Cruise Missile Combat Control System Mark 1." Department of the Navy, 1989.

Wells, Anthony. "Real Time Targeting: Myth or Reality." *Proceedings of the United States Naval Institute,* August 2001.

Wells, Anthony. "US Naval Power and the Pursuit of Peace in an Era of International Terrorism and Weapons of Mass Destruction." *The Submarine Review*, October 2002.

Wells, Anthony. "Limited Objective Experiment ZERO." The Naval Air Systems Command, July 2002, Department of the Navy.

Wells, Anthony. "Transformation—Some Insights and Observations for the Royal Navy from Across the Atlantic." *The Naval Review*, August 2003.

Wells, Anthony. "Distributed Data Analysis with Bayesian Networks: A Preliminary Study for the Non- Proliferation of Radioactive Devices." With Dr. Farid Dowla and Dr. G. Larson, December 2003, The Lawrence Livermore National Laboratory.

Wells, Anthony. "Fiber Reinforced Pumice Protective Barriers: To mitigate the effects of suicide and truck bombs." Final Report and recommendations. With Professor Vistasp Kharbari, Professor of Structural Engineering, University of California, San Diego, August 2006. For the Naval Air Systems Command, Department of the Navy. Washington DC.

Wells, Anthony. "Weapon Target Centric Model. Preliminary Modules and Applications. Two Volumes." Principal Executive Officer Submarines, August 2007, Naval Sea Systems Command, Department of the Navy.

Wells, Anthony. "They Did Not Die in Vain. USS Liberty Incident—Some Additional Perspectives." *Proceedings of the United States Naval Institute,* March 2005.

Wells, Anthony. "Royal Navy at the Crossroads: Turn the Strategic Tide. A Way to Implement a Lasting Vision." *The Naval Review*, November 2010.

Wells, Anthony. "The Royal Navy is Key to Britain's Security Strategy." *Proceedings of the United States Naval Institute*, December 2010.

Wells, Anthony. "The Survivability of the Royal Navy and a new Enlightened British Defense Strategy." *The Submarine Review*, January 2011.

Wells, Anthony. "A Strategy in East Asia that can Endure." *Proceedings of the United States Naval Institute*, May 2011. Reprinted in *The Naval Review*, August 2011, by kind permission of the United States Naval Institute.

Wells, Anthony. "Tactical Decision Aid: Multi intelligence capability for National, Theater, and Tactical Intelligence in real time across geographic pace and time." May 2012, Department of the Navy and US National Intelligence community.

Wells, Anthony. "Submarine Industrial Base Model: Key industrial base model for the US Virginia Class nuclear powered attack submarine." With Dr. Carol V. Evans. Principal Executive Officer Submarines, Naval Sea Systems Command, Department of the Navy.

Wells, Anthony. "The United States Navy, Jordan, and a Long-Term Israeli-Palestinian Security Agreement." *The Submarine Review*, Spring 2013.

Wells, Anthony. "Admiral Sir Herbert Richmond: What would he think, write and action today?" *The Naval Review Centenary Edition*, February 2013.

Wells, Anthony. "Jordan, Israel, and US Need to cooperate for Missile Defense." *United States Naval Institute News*, March 2013.

Wells, Anthony. "A Tribute to Admiral Sir John 'Sandy' Woodward." *United States Naval Institute News,* August 2013.

Wells, Anthony. "USS Liberty Document Center." Edited with Thomas Schaaf. A document web site produced by SiteWhirks,

Warrenton, Virginia. September 2013. This site was transferred to the United States Library of Congress in April 2018, to be maintained in perpetuity for the benefit of scholars, analysts, and historians. USSLibertyDocumentCenter.org.

Wells, Anthony. "The Future of ISIS: A Joint US–Russian Assessment." With Dr. Andrey Chuprygin. *The Naval Review*, May 2015.

Wells, Anthony. *A Tale of Two Navies. Geopolitics, Technology, and Strategy in the United States Navy and the Royal Navy, 1960–2015*. Annapolis, Maryland: United States Naval Institute Press, 2017.

Wells, Anthony & Phillips, James W, Captain US Navy (retired). "Put the Guns in a Box." *Proceedings of the United States Naval Institute*, Annapolis, Maryland, June 2018.

Wemyss, D. E. G. *Walker's Group in the Western Approaches*. Liverpool: Liverpool Post and Echo, 1948.

Werner, H. A. *Iron Coffin. A Personal Account of German U-boat Battles of World War Two*. London: Arthur Barker, 1969.

West, N. *A Matter of Trust: MI5 1945–1972*. London: Weidenfeld and Nicholson, 1982.

West, N. *GCHQ: The Secret Wireless War, 1900–1986*. London: Weidenfeld and Nicholson, 1986.

West, N. *The Secret War for the Falklands*. London: Little Brown, 1997.

West, N. *Venona*. London: Harper Collins, 1999.

West, N. *At Her Majesty's Secret Service: The Chiefs of Britain's Intelligence Agency, MI6*. London: Greenhill Books, 2006.

Westad, Odd Arne. *The Cold War: A World History*. Oxford: Oxford University Press, 2017.

Wheatley, R. *Operation Sea Lion. German Plans for the Invasion of England, 1939–1942*. Oxford: Clarendon Press, 1958.

Wilkinson, N. *Secrecy and the Media: The Official History of the UK's D-Notice System*. London: Routledge, 2009.

Wilmot, C. *The Struggle for Europe*. London: Harper Collins, 1952.

Wilson, H. *The Labour Government 1964–1970: A Personal Record.* London: Michael Joseph, 1971.

Winterbotham, F. *The Ultra Secret.* London: Weidenfeld & Nicholson, 1974.

Wohlstetter, R. *Pearl Harbor, Warning and Decision.* London: Methuen, 1957.

Wolin, S. and R. M. Slusser. *The Soviet Secret Police.* London: Methuen, 1957.

Womack, Helen, ed. *Undercover Lives: Soviet Spies in the Cities of the World.* London: Orion Publishing Company, 1998.

Wood, D. and D. Dempster. *The Narrow Margin.* London: Hutchinson, 1961.

Woodward, Admiral Sir John "Sandy." *One Hundred Days. The Memoirs of the Falklands Battle Group Commander.* With Patrick Robinson. Annapolis, Maryland: United States Naval Institute Press, 1992.

Woodward, L. *My Life as a Spy.* London: Macmillan, 2005.

Wright, P, with Greengrass, Paul. *Spycatcher. The Candid Autobiography of a Senior Intelligence Officer.* New York: Viking, 1987.

Wylde, N., ed. *The Story of Brixmis, 1946–1990.* Arundel: Brixmis Association, 1993.

Young, J. and J. Kent. *International Relations Since 1945.* Oxford: Oxford University Press, 2004.

Young, J. W. *The Labour Governments, 1964–1970: International Policy.* Manchester: Manchester University Press, 2003.

Zimmerman, B. *France, 1944. The Fatal Decisions.* London: Michael Joseph, 1956.

ABOUT THE AUTHOR

Dr. Anthony R. Wells (Taken in Prague, Czech Republic)

Anthony Wells is unique insofar as he is the only living person to have worked for British intelligence as a British citizen and US intelligence as a US citizen, and to have also served in uniform at sea and ashore with both the Royal Navy and the US Navy. He is a 50-year veteran of the Five Eyes intelligence community. In 2017 he was the Keynote Speaker on board HMS Victory in Portsmouth, England, to commemorate the 100th anniversary of the famous Zimmermann Telegram intelligence coup by "Blinker Hall" and his Room 40 team in British Naval Intelligence. The guest of honor was Her Royal Highness Princess Anne, with the Five Eyes community, past and present, represented from the United States, the United Kingdom, Canada, Australia, and New Zealand. Dr. Wells, or Commander Wells, was trained and mentored in the late 1960s by the very best of the World War II intelligence community, including Sir Harry Hinsley, the famous Bletchley Park code breaker, official historian of British Intelligence in the Second World War, Master of St. John's College, Cambridge, and Vice Chancellor of Cambridge University. Sir Harry Hinsley introduced Dr. Wells to the Enigma data before it became public knowledge. Dr. Wells received his PhD in War Studies from King's College, University of London, in 1972. He holds Bachelor and Masters Degrees from the University of Durham, and a Masters degree from the London School of Economics. He was trained at Britannia Royal Naval College, Dartmouth and received his advanced training at the School of Maritime Operations.

He was called to the Bar by Lincoln's Inn in November, 1980. Anthony Wells has four children and eight grandchildren, and lives on his farm in Virginia. He is a Member of the Naval Order of the United States and was appointed an Honorary Crew Member of USS Liberty by the USS Liberty Veterans Association. USS Liberty is the most highly decorated warship in the history of the US Navy for a single action, attacked by Israeli air and surface forces on August 8, 1967 in the eastern Mediterranean. Dr Wells is the third Chairman of the USS Liberty Alliance, succeeding the late Admiral Thomas Moorer, former Chairman of the US Joint Chiefs of Staff and Chief of Naval Operations, and the late Rear Admiral Clarence "Mark" Hill, former distinguished US naval aviator and battle group commander. He is a retired US National Ski Patroller and Instructor, and a Life Member and former President of The Plains, Virginia, Volunteer Fire & Rescue Company. Wells is an FAA Commercial pilot with single and multi engine, land and sea, instrument, and flight instructor Ratings.

He is a Senior Member of Number 60 Squadron of the Civil Air Patrol. Dr. Wells was the Technical Director of Fleet Battle Experiments ALPHA and BRAVO in the Third Fleet, United States Pacific Fleet. He was the Chief Executive Officer of TKC International LLC, a specialist company supporting the US Intelligence Community and Department of Defense, for twenty-five years. He held Top Secret SCI and Special Access Clearances.

Anthony Wells' Publications:

Literary Awards:

In 2013 & 2017 the United States Submarine League presented Dr. Anthony R. Wells with Literary Awards for Articles in The Submarine Review.

Books:

German Public Opinion and Hitler's Policies, 1933-39. 1968. Electronic version available at Durham University Library, UK – access www to Durham University Library and enter data base with title and/or author name. Electronic and hard copy versions available.

Studies in British Naval Intelligence, 1880-1945. 1972. Electronic version available via the www British Library (ETHOS), and also King's College, London – www and then enter the data base with title and/or author name. Electronic and hard copy versions available. Also simply enter title, and by Anthony Roland Wells and a www edition is available on line.

Training and the Achievement of Management Objectives, the Solution of Management Problems, and as an Instrument of Organizational Change. 1974. The London School of Economics and Political Science.

Technical Change and British Naval Policy. Edited by Bryan Ranft, Hodder and Stoughton, London, 1977, and Holmes and Meier, New York, NY.

War and Society. Edited by Brian Bond and Ian Roy, Croom Helm, London, 1977, and Holmes and Meier, New York, NY.

Soviet Naval Diplomacy. Edited by B. Dismukes and J. McConnell, Pergamon Press, 1979.

The Soviet and Other Communist Navies. Edited by James George, US Naval Institute Press, Annapolis, Maryland, 1986.

Black Gold Finale. A novel. Dorrance Publishing Company, 2009.

The Golden Few. A novel. Dorrance Publishing Company, 2012.

A Tale of Two Navies: Geopolitics, Technology, and Strategy in the United States and the Royal Navy, 1960-2015. US Naval Institute Press, Annapolis, Maryland, January, 2017.

Between Five Eyes. Casemate Publishers, Oxford, UK & Havertown, Pennsylvania, September, 2020.

Room39 and the Lisbon Connection. A novel. Xlibris, Bloomington, Indiana, June, 2021

Crossroads in Time Philby & Angleton. A Story of Treachery. A novel. Palmetto Publishing, Charleston, South Carolina, 2022 and Austin Macauley Publishers, London, 2022.

Gone to Earth A Young American Woman Disappears in the South Pacific. Based on a True Story. A novel. Xlibris, Bloomington, Indiana, 2022.

How Strategic Airpower has Tipped the Balance on the Global Stage From the 100th Bomb Group to the Falklands and Beyond. With Commander Nigel "Sharkey" Ward, DSC, AFC, Royal Navy (Retired). Pen and Sword Books, Barnsley, UK, 2024.

Guarding against Extremism in the 21st Century A Lesson from the Past German Public Opinion and Hitler's Policies 1933-1939. XLibris, Bloomington, Indiana, 2023.

Intrepid's Footsteps Sustaining US-UK Intelligence in an Era of Global Challenges. A Personal Memoire. Xlibris Bloomington, Indiana, 2023.

From Blinker Hall to Room 39 British Naval Intelligence 1880-1945. Austin Macauley Publishers, London, 2024.

Never Too Late A Story for Every Parent and Young Person. Based on a True Story. To be published in 2024.

In the Pursuit of Peace Science Law and Art To be published in 2024

Articles

Admirals Hall and Godfrey - Doyens of Naval Intelligence (Two Parts). The Naval Review, 1973.

Staff Training and the Royal Navy (Two Parts). The Naval Review 1975, 1976.

The 1967 June War: Soviet Naval Diplomacy and the Sixth Fleet - A Reappraisal. Center for Naval Analyses, Arlington, Virginia. Professional Paper 204, October 1977.

The Center for Naval Analyses. Professional Paper Number 197, December 1977. Department of the Navy, Washington DC, Center for Naval Analyses.

The Soviet Navy in the Arctic and North Atlantic. National Defense, February, 1986.

Soviet Submarine Prospects 1985-2000. Submarine Review, January 1986.

A New Defense Strategy for Britain. Proceedings of the United States Naval Institute, March 1987.

Presence and Military Strategies of the USSR in the Arctic. Quebec Center for International Relations, Laval University, 1986.

Real Time Targeting: Myth or Reality. Proceedings of the United States Naval Institute, August, 2001.

Missing Magics Machine Material. New Insights on December 7, 1941 and Relevance for Today's Navy. The Submarine Review, April 2003.

US Naval Power and the Pursuit of Peace in an Era of International Terrorism and Weapons of Mass Destruction. The Submarine Review, October 2002.

Transformation - Some Insights and Observations for the Royal Navy from Across the Atlantic. The Naval Review, August 2003.

They Did Not Die In Vain. USS Liberty Incident - Some Additional Perspectives. Proceedings of the United States Naval Institute, March, 2005

Royal Navy at the Crossroads: Turn the Strategic Tide. A Way to Implement a Lasting Vision. The Naval Review, November, 2010

The Royal Navy is Key to Britain's Security Strategy. Proceedings of the United States Naval Institute, December, 2010

The Survivability of the Royal Navy and a New Enlightened British Defense Strategy. The Submarine Review, January, 2011

A Strategy in East Asia that can Endure. Proceedings of the United States Naval Institute, May, 2011

A Strategy in East Asia that can Endure. The Naval Review, August 2011. Reprinted by kind permission of the United States Naval Institute.

The United States Navy, Jordan, and a Long Term Israeli-Palestinian Security Agreement. The Submarine Review, Spring 2012

Admiral Sir Herbert Richmond: What would he think, write and action today? The Naval Review, February 2013 – Lead article in the Centenary Edition of The Naval Review.

Postscript to Missing Magics Machine Material – Tribute to a Great Submariner: Captain Edward Beach, US Navy. The Submarine Review, 2013

Jordan, Israel, and US Need to Cooperate for Missile Defense. USNI News, March 26, 2103.

A Tribute to Admiral Sir John "Sandy" Woodward. USNI News, August 8, 2013

USS LIBERTY Document Center. Edited by Anthony Wells and Thomas Schaaf. A web site produced by SiteWhirks, Inc., Warrenton, Virginia. September 2013. In April, 2017 this website was transferred to the Library of Congress for permanent safekeeping for the use of future scholars and researchers.

The Future of ISIS: A Joint US-Russian Assessment. With Dr. Andrey Chuprygin. The Naval Review, May 2015

The Zimmermann Telegram: 100th Anniversary. The Naval Review, February, 2017 & The Submarine Review 2017.

Put The Guns in a Box: With Captain J W Phillips, US Navy retired. Proceedings of the US Naval Institute, June, 2018.

Quo Vadis China? A View from Across the Atlantic. Part 1. The Naval Review. November, 2019.

Quo Vadis China? The Submarine Review, December, 2019.

USS Amberjack and the Attack on USS Liberty: With Mr. Larry Taylor, ST1 USS Amberjack. US Naval Institute Naval History Blog, January 7, 2020

USS Amberjack & the Attack on USS Liberty. With Mr. Larry Taylor. The Submarine Review. March, 2020.

The UK's Strategic Defense & Security Review, A US Perspective. The Submarine Review. June, 2020.

The United Kingdom Needs a Maritime Strategy. The Naval Review, August, 2020.

Submarines and the Ring of Fire in the Indo Pacific Theater: A Strategic Analysis. The Submarine Review, December, 2020.

UK's Defense & Security Review – Some Final Observations: The Naval Review. Autumn 2020.

A Brave New World of Next Generation Technologies: Warship World: Volume 17, Number 2, January/February, 2021.

To Honor The Last Nuremburg Prosecutor: Proceedings of the United States Naval Institute May, 2021, Annapolis, Maryland.

The United Nations Convention on the Law of the Sea and the United States Navy: US Naval Institute Blog, June, 2021.

Is There a Need for a New Generation of Submarine Officers who are Intelligence Trained and Experienced beyond Current Levels? & How Might We Learn from the Past? The Submarine Review, June, 2021.

Behind the Five Eyes: Counsel Magazine (Justice Matters: Spotlight section), the monthly magazine of the Bar of England & Wales, London, UK, July, 2021.

Deterrence is Key in a US & Allied Global Maritime Strategy. Submarine Review, June, 2023.

Letter from The Plains: A monthly article in the Middleburg Eccentric, Virginia, since 2016 to November, 2022.

Reports:

NATO and US Carrier Deployment Policies. Center for Naval Analyses, Arlington, Virginia, February 1977.

NATO and US Carrier Deployment Policies, Formation of a New Standing Naval Strike Force in NATO. Center for Naval Analyses, Arlington, Virginia, April 1977.

Sea War '85 Scenario. With Captain John L. Underwood, USN. Center for Naval Analyses, Arlington, Virginia, June 1977.

Submarine Construction Program for the State of Sabah, Malaysia. RDA Contract TR-188600-OOl, December 1984. Chief Minister of Sabah, Malaysia and Government of Malaysia.

The Application of Drag Reduction and Boundary Layer Control Technologies in an Experimental Program. January 1985. For the Chief Naval Architect, Vickers Shipbuilding and Engineering Ltd, Barrow-in-Furness, UK.

The Strategic Importance and Advantages of Labuan, Federal Malaysian Territory, as a Naval Base with Special Reference to its Capabilities as the Royal Malaysian Navy Submarine Base, March 1985. Chief Minister of Sabah, Malaysia and Government of Malaysia.

Preliminary Overview of Soviet Merchant Ships in Anti-SSBN Operations and Soviet Merchant Ships and Submarine Masking. (Department of the Navy Contract N00016-85-C-0204).

SSBN Port Egress and the Non-Commercial Activities of the Soviet Merchant Fleet: Concepts of Operation and War Orders for Current and Future Anti-SSBN Operations. (Department of the Navy Contract 136400).

Overview Study of the Maritime Aspects of the Nuclear Balance in the European Theater (Department of Energy Study for the European Conflict Analysis Project). October 1986.

Soviet Submarine Warfare Strategy Assessment and Future US Submarine and Anti-Submarine Warfare Technologies (Defense Advanced Research Projects Agency, March 1988), RDA Contract 146601).

Limited Objective Experiment ZERO, July 2000. The Naval Air Systems Command, US Navy, Department of Defense. 2002.

Operational factors Associated with the Software Nuclear Safety Analysis for the UGM-109A Tomahawk Submarine-Launched Land Attack Cruise Missile Combat Control System Mark I. United States Navy and Logicon Inc., 1989.

Operation Bahrain, March 2003. The Assistant Director of Central Intelligence, the Central Intelligence Agency.

Distributed Data Analysis with Bayesian Networks: A Preliminary Study for Non-Proliferation of Radioactive Devices, December 2003 (with F. Dowla and G. Larson). The Lawrence Livermore National Laboratory, Livermore, California, December 2003.

FIBER REINFORCED PUMICE PROTECTIVE BARRIERS – To Mitigate the Effects of Suicide and Truck Bombs. Final Report and Recommendations. United States Navy, Washington DC. With Professor Vistasp Kharbari, Professor of Structural Engineering, University of California, San Diego. August, 2006.

WEAPON TARGET CENTRIC MODEL: Preliminary Modules and Applications, in Two Volumes. United States Navy, Principal Executive Officer Submarines, Washington DC, August, 2007.

TACTICAL DECISION AID (TDA): Multi intelligence capability for National, Theater, and Tactical intelligence in real time across geographic space and time. The National Intelligence Community, Washington DC, May 2012.

SUBMARINE INDUSTRIAL BASE MODEL: Key industrial base model for the US VIRGINIA Class nuclear powered attack submarine, Principal Executive Officer Submarines, Washington Navy Yard, Washington DC, October 2012.

Manuals:

Astro-Navigation: A Programmed Course in 6 Volumes for Training UK and Commonwealth Naval Officers in the Use of Astronomical Navigation at Sea. Royal Navy, Ministry of Defence, UK, 1969.

The Battle of Trafalgar: A Programmed Course in one Volume in Naval Strategy and Tactics. Royal Navy, Ministry of Defence, 1969.

The Double Cross System: A Programmed Course In one Volume for British, Foreign and Commonwealth Naval Officers Attending the Royal Naval Staff College, Greenwich, UK. Royal Navy, Ministry of Defence, 1973.

Airborne Mine Clearance

Streak Tube Imaging LIDAR

Magic Lantern Program

Tritium Micro sphere Technology

Classified Applications of the Naval Simulation System

Naval Surface Fire Support and the Extended Range Guided Munition (ERGM)

Non Acoustic Antisubmarine Warfare

Battlefield Awareness and Data Dissemination (BADD Program)

Joint Stars Program Special Applications

Naval Fires Network

Littoral Surveillance System

Fleet Battle Experiment Operations (Technical Director FBE Alpha and FBE Bravo) Third Fleet, US Pacific Fleet

Ocean Surveillance (radar and optics)

Multi Spectral Applications

Space Based Sensors and Surveillance

Microwave Radiometry Applications

Detection, Locating and Tracking

Clandestine Operations and Intelligence Collection Operations

Support to Special Forces

Special Submarine Operations

Tagging Tracking and Surveillance

Battlespace Shaping and Real Time Targeting

Covert and Clandestine Operations against Weapons of Mass Destruction and Other major threats to US Security

Special Sensor Technology

Covert & Overt Operations Planning and Execution

Reports and MOUs for Commander-in-Chief and Secretary level actions

Airborne Infrared Measurement System

Stealth and Counter Stealth

Counter Intelligence Operations
Tactical Exploitation System and Joint Fires Network
Asymmetric Warfare Initiative – 2003
Hairy Buffalo Program
Tracking of the al Qai'da Terrorist Network and Operations
Tactical Decision Aid (TDA) for Submarine ISR operations
Advanced Cyber Attack and Defense Technologies and Operations
Shrouded Lightning Special Program
Non Linear Junction Radar and Adaptive Regenerative Controller Special Program
Special Program in Jordan
Special Program in Malaysia
Special Program in Bahrain
Special Program in Abu Dhabi
Special Program in Saudi Arabia
Special Program with Commander United States Pacific Fleet
Special Tests at the US Naval Air Station Patuxent River, Maryland, September 2012
LISAC Special Program
Applications of the Robust Laser Interferometry (RLI) system and technology
Special Support to a combined Cheltenham UK and Maryland US Group
Special Support for Indo-Pacific Operations

Classified Titles & Publications:

1968-2018 Dr. Wells has been the author, lead author, or a key author of multiple highly classified Codeword documents at the Top Secret SCI level in both the United Kingdom and the United States.

The End

www.ingramcontent.com/pod-product-compliance
Lightning Source LLC
Chambersburg PA
CBHW051043250726
48656CB00001B/124